The Mindful, Intentional YOU

Being conscious in an unconscious world

Daily Motivations from my Book, Blog & Brain

KIMBERLY MITCHELL

Copyright © 2018 by Kimberly Mitchell

All rights reserved. No portion of this book may be used or reproduced in any form or by any means, electronic or mechanical, including photocopying, recording, or by any information storage and retrieval system without written permission from the publisher, except in the case of brief quotations embodied in reviews. For information contact White Orchid Publishing, LLC at www.lovingwithpurpose.org or kmitchell@lovingwithpurpose.org.

Published by WHITE ORCHID PUBLISHING, LLC, Hamilton, OH

First paperback edition. White Orchid Publishing, LLC, 2018

WHITE ORCHID PUBLISHING, LLC is a trade name of Kimberly Mitchell

Grateful acknowledgement is made to the following:
Stock photography courtesy of White Orchid Publishing, LLC.
Authors of statistics, tales, and quotes shared in this book are given credit when known. All others are noted as unknown.

White Orchid Publishing, LLC or the author assumes no liability or responsibility for damage or injury to you, other persons, or property arising from any use of any product, information, idea, or instruction contained in the content provided to you through this book. This publication is designed to provide accurate and authoritative information with regard to the subject matter covered. It is sold with the understanding that the publisher is not engaged in rendering legal, accounting, or other professional advice. If legal advice or other expert assistance is required, the services of a competent professional person should be sought.

For information regarding bulk purchases or any other needs, please contact White Orchid Publishing, LLC at www.lovingwithpurpose.org or kmitchell@lovingwithpurpose.org

Printed in the United States of America.

Library of Congress Control Number: 2018904919
ISBN 978-0-9825964-3-2

DEDICATION

*This book is dedicated to my dearest friend and bright light, Patricia Schiering;
my sister soul who always seeks the brighter side of life.
Thank you for always helping me to "turn it around."*

ACKNOWLEDGMENTS

One thing that life never fails to show us…it never stops changing. I know I've seen even more change in me, and in life, since my first book. While most of my belief system has remained intact, there has been some shifting and tweaking as I moved along; opening new ways to think about life.

For instance, when I receive new information that in some way challenges my beliefs, I go back to the drawing board, so to speak. I determine what I need to do to make this life…my life…get back in balance. Just as new generations bring clarity or concern with their different beliefs, I, too, have continued to learn and grow!

So, for that reason, I acknowledge me, and my willingness to continue unfolding and expanding myself and my relationships.

I dedicate this writing to my dearest friend, Patti Schiering, who always looks for the brightest light in every given situation. When one of us encounters some sort of personal turmoil, we talk the other one through the matter. We do it with grace, compassion, and the knowledge that this, too, shall pass.

And, because of this friend, and her gentle, loving wisdom, I continually find myself getting back to a peaceful place. Today, I can gather up my happiness and hope; all with less effort and time. For this and so many other reasons, I am thankful for her love and lessons.

Patti is the type of friend who is always loyal, genuine, willful, kind, and honest with me. I hope everyone is as fortunate to have even one friend as loving as she has been to me.

I would also like to thank my sister, Kathy, and the *OMC* gals (you know who you are), for helping me get the best version of my writing out into the world. Your feedback has been greatly appreciated.

CONTENTS

	Introduction	i
1	Think it Over; Then...Think Again	1
2	Face to Face With You & Your Choices	19
3	Stand Out Above the Rest	45
4	Conscious Change	63
5	Cause & Effect	93
6	Intentional Gratitude	105
7	The Give & Take of Relating in Relationships	123
8	The Audit of Your Attitude	159

Helpful Resources
About the Author

"Seek first to understand, then to be understood."
~ Stephen Covey

INTRODUCTION

Years ago, when I started writing, I had to consider my target audience, so I would speak directly to a certain group of people. I started writing to men in a humorous way about chivalry. Then, I realized I probably wouldn't reach most of them so I turned the book around. I still want to write that book, but for now it will have to wait.

It's not that men don't get it. In fact, quite a few have read my book. Still, getting my thoughts to a larger number of readers was important to me, and they simply don't gravitate toward this type of book.

Even with the idea of writing to men, my goal has always been for a woman to be treated well…as she should. When a woman is on the receiving end of respect, she learns to *expect* more for herself. She begins to feel and believe what is true and knowing…that she is awesome!

So I switched my thoughts to young women. I used a more thoughtful and attentive style of writing so I could reach those who needed inspiration and flexible rules. I would share ideas that she could apply to her and her relationships. I wanted her to improve her life, by helping her connect with the *thought* that she is unique and special…and she should *expect* to be treated as such.

I knew transition could not come without self-realization and compromise. Change would require her to make a return on her investment. Not only would she have to learn more about herself, she has to discover how to give herself to others. She also needs to anticipate getting more. More of what she needs from those around her.

The conclusion I came to is a woman needs to focus her attention on continually living her life the way she desires and deserves. She does this by giving and receiving in a way that brings her happiness, contentment, and peace.

So…your first lesson in your walk of mindfulness is to be considerate, compromising, compassionate, and humble. Most importantly, be intentional with yourself, your words, and actions. Nothing good comes from getting angry, frustrated, mean, or disrespectful.

You'll see that reaching your solutions and goals requires none of that negativity. An intentional person knows *how* to stand up for themselves…and without all of the drama usually connected to it. It's only necessary to stand strong in a productive and mindful way.

Clearly, no one has all the answers, this is true. No one gives completely of themselves one-hundred percent *all* of the time. We encounter roadblocks that challenge us to step up and do or say the right thing. And we don't always get it right!

When you determine what's missing in your life, there, you'll begin to identify with what you need to do, say, or be. The awesome part of growth is recognizing that singular moment where you took a brand new step. When you kept your mind quiet, your mouth shut, or you said and did all the right things.

What I learned in the process, thanks to my readers, is that my audience goes beyond the eighteen to thirty-year-old gal. Instead, my writing reaches all women (and some men) in need of assistance; about personal development, religion, finance, abuse, and yes, dating and relationships! A woman's life never stops changing…and those changes come at every age in life.

As for me, I still need to reconnect with the same advice I've held dear for so long. I will never finish reinventing my life. Although, sometimes it's merely a matter of being reminded what is actually important in the grand scheme of things! In short, I need to know what makes me 'me.'

Take this time to learn more about you. Be more informed about your loved ones in a deeper way. See them differently. You might even see yourself reconnecting with that one special person standing right in front of you; your sibling, son, parent, or mate! When love shows its defining qualities, anything is possible. If you believe that, life can unfold in ways you never imagined.

I begin each chapter with an Afterthought from me; notes on what you'll read. Then, I spent months tweaking the sections and articles that I've written in the past. With more time and age behind me, life gave me more perspective and insight. I take this time to share those thoughts with you, as well as, give you the best of my book and blog, *Loving with Purpose*.

As for my future, I will share other subject matter with you (relationships, family, work, money, religion, finance, abuse, and dating) in other books. But for now, I want you to focus on this specific topic…being intentional. Call it what you like; intentional, mindfulness, or conscious thinking. What I do know is that you will discover more about yourself, and how *you* can make all the difference.

Happy reading!

The Mindful, Intentional YOU

Being conscious in an unconscious world

Foreword

As stated before, early on in my writing process I knew I had to write to women. I would like to reach men, and I do, but women are usually the ones looking to improve themselves and their relationships. Because I switched to talking to women, my writing took on a life of its own. I offered helpful advice about her, her consciousness, dating, marriage, children, abuse, and religion…just to name a few.

After I finished my bundle of love (*Loving with Purpose*), I started to wonder if the content was too much information for some readers. Perhaps, I should break it down into more specific topics.

So I started separating! I took chunks of writing from my book and blog and created a book for each subject matter! While the others are still in the works, this one is on being intentional. I chose this topic first because I believe *intention* is the foundation necessary to obtain knowledge from the rest. Each book allows you, the reader, to get more in depth on one particular subject matter; the area of your life that you'd like to improve upon.

These daily motivations came from my *book, blog, and brain*. You have my afterthoughts and revisions, all to make the reading journey as nice as possible for you…the reader. I hope to capture your attention, by topic, so you get what you want out of *your* life.

1
Think it Over; Then...Think Again

"I'm a secure, uncertain, mindful, conscious, purposeful, error making, lesson learning, empowered, and creative woman. I'm always working on me and doing the best I can..."in the moment."

~ K Mitchell

AFTERTHOUGHT

So what made me write in the first place? Let me tell you. My journey all began with me trying to find my purpose. I was at a crossroads in my life. I left my corporate job, got married, and realized I had lost a part of myself in the process. From there, my passion grew into wanting to reach young people. I wanted to somehow change their lives. I discovered writing was a great tool to accomplish such a task, and I truly enjoyed sharing my thoughts with the rest of the world.

My purpose: keep people from going through some of the drama that can creep in and enter without your approval. In my life, I know I could have handled certain situations better than I did. If only I had reached out for some advice. Maybe…just maybe…I could have gotten through some of the hardships much sooner.

I am grateful for the lesson of intention. When I think of the countless hours, days, and weeks I have added back to my future, by *not* holding myself down during difficult times, I know mindfulness is a true blessing. Today, I understand how to work quickly through the chaos so I can spring back to life. You have heard it called by many names; mindfulness, awareness, being conscious, or some other label. Whatever you call it, it's a blessing when we are self-aware. Everyone goes through tough times, but with the right tools, you get back to a peaceful beginning much sooner than ever before.

> *"Everything is energy and that's all there is to it. Match the frequency of the reality you want and you cannot help but get that reality. It can be no other way. This is not philosophy. This is physics."*
> ~ Albert Einstein

So let's reach deeper. Let's probe into the thought process. Devote some time to looking at the lessons I've acquired over the years. Let's see how others handled life challenges, too. My hope is that through my sharing you reap the benefits…for you and your future.

BEING CONSCIOUS IN
AN UNCONSCIOUS WORLD

Everyone seems to be in such a hurry these days; trying to get ahead, pushing the clock, checking into social media and checking out of human interaction. When do we make a conscious effort to be present?

Being intentional requires easy and challenging efforts. Believe it or not, the easiest portion is being intentional. You decide at any moment to be aware of what's going on around you. The harder part is controlling your mind. Creating that *new habit* requires effort and sustainability.

What you'll discover about being conscious is a change in how you feel, act, and many times how others perceive you. The change doesn't come all at once. Some insights never occur. Still, you will recognize a change in one way or another.

Being intentional (in a positive sense) is the best way to create happiness in your home and abroad. When you consciously speak and act, you know *why* you are saying and doing something. Let me share a few instances on how to become more intentional.

For starters, you can attempt to be intentional in everything you say and do: your actions, speaking, *and* thinking. Whew! That's a lot of effort! It's not easy motivating yourself to live with intent in every single second of the day and in everything you say and do.

What about a particular action or event being accomplished with intention? That is a good start! Consider the action of hiking. You have the choice to simply walk, look around, check the time, or talk on the phone. Or you can experience hiking.

With that first step, take in the view, be mindful of each step, and listen to every noise. Hear the crunching of the breaking branches under your feet as you walk along. Watch the squirrel or other small creature scurrying around for food or other supplies. With practice, you can hear everything going on around you. It becomes your personal setting. Then, there is the silence within those sounds. Become aware of the crispness of the air, the leaves falling toward the ground, and the flutter of a bird's wings. Then again, you could just stop and take in the depth of the spot you find yourself standing. Simply put, losing your thoughts and focusing in on the moment.

In every occurrence there is something deeper than whatever is happening in front of you. You can be in the midst of a conversation with someone, or in the stillness of nature, and still not get to intention. There is a deeper, more impressive portion that's not quickly revealed. You just have to look for it.

One way to move toward conscious thinking is to look at every situation you encounter without judgement. Instead, question why an incident is occurring. Devote some time to reflect on the occurrence so you can better understand.

Specifically, look at moments which require consciousness to its fullest possible extent; like a time when conflict reared its ugly head. You have at least two choices in that instant and how you handle yourself can mean everything. You could calmly *seek first to understand* their position (and feelings), or you could rapidly come to your own conclusions, screaming, or storming off. All of the latter choices can make a bad moment even worse.

Learn to look at both sides of everything. When someone disagrees with you, consider the idea that maybe they are right. At the very least, ask yourself if it really matters who is right? Honestly, being right is overrated many times. People don't have to agree, but they do need to be respectful toward each other. Determine how important the moment is to you and then proceed.

When new situations arise, relationships can really get botched up if you don't approach your newfound knowledge with some clarity of mind. You may think you have the answers to all of the issues infused into your little world, but you don't. You can't always be the fixer of conflict. There are times when you need to sit back and reflect.

On a personal note, I can't help but snicker when thinking about how much I thought I knew back in my younger years. No one could tell me anything about anything. I guess that's why I ended up leaving home so young. Home was a good place so I had no big reason to go. I was bullheaded and ready to conquer the world.

I was married at seventeen, had a baby by nineteen, and divorced by twenty. Now, does that sound smart to you? There's nothing like spiraling backwards with no safety net to catch you! And while I don't regret my choices because I am so blessed to have my son, I could have taken a kinder route to get to the good stuff.

What I do know is there is nothing like the arrival of that first bill to make a person sit up and take notice. Funny how independence can slap you right in the face when you aren't paying attention to your choices. I learned quickly what it meant to be independent. Unfortunately, it took me a lot longer to see how my choices were creating my life…and my son's life.

If only I would have listened to the people who knew more than I did. Perhaps, I could have saved myself tons of mistakes. I could have learned much sooner than I did; from my first step as a youngster till today! Yes, I still learn today. Everyone should.

> *"You can learn from other people's mistakes.*
> *You don't have to make them yourself."*
> ~ Bre Payton

So while I could have taken a kinder route in life, there are moments in my past I would never change. Even if I had to relive the pain that came with some of my choices, I wouldn't change it. Where I've been has prepared me for who I am today. My past gave me who I have in life, and it made me a better woman. Now, I am the one who is reaching out, wanting to help others make better choices…sooner.

https://thefederalist.com/author/bre-payton/

HOW THOUGHTS PLAY AN ACTIVE ROLE

We are living in interesting times. There are more opportunities to create change in our lives, and even more doors opening that were sealed in the past. For instance, women today have much more influence in every aspect of the world than they used to. Today, we're seen as experts in many fields: scientists, doctors, and astronauts. Not long ago, we were only seen as secretaries, factory workers, and housekeepers.

Today, men and women are also more open-minded to possibilities that can't be seen or even touched. For example, people who believe in spiritual powers can talk more openly about their thoughts. They are more accepted by others as real possibilities. In the past, these beliefs would have been seen as strange and even crazy. Now, society recognizes that thoughts, words, and attitudes can play an active role in a desired outcome.

Many of us would like to live in a faultless world, but as you know, that is not possible. Creating conditions for success, through positive energy and actions, can inspire real change in a less than impeccable atmosphere. Set the scene for yourself by focusing on the positive and leaving as much of the negative behind as possible.

If you hold onto a problem, the best solution to a better mood is consistency in how you handle the problem…in the best possible way. Consistency requires you to create the steps in your mind, follow them, and then release the problem. Here are the steps for resolving conflict within your mind:

- First, see if there is anything you need to do about the problem
- Formulate a solution (when possible)
- Take action (when needed)
- Pray for help (always)
- Then, release the pressure of wondering if there is anything else you need to do about that particular situation

While you go along problem-solving the issues that come up, there will be difficult days in the mix. Days filled with tears and sorrow, and even pain. Still, what you experience or suffer *is* the lesson.

As you learn to become more conscious, you'll come back with even more strength and perseverance, for the greater good. You'll have the power to see the good out of every bad situation. You know there is a lesson to be learned.

You will have a searchable spirit; one that allows you to view scenarios from a perspective different than your own. You will see every issue as an *opportunity* to handle controversy in a better way. Just think and react to every occasion in a fresh, new way. Different than you ever have before!

A lot can be absorbed through examination of each issue you encounter. Learn to examine your thought process and control your emotions about the issue at hand. Avoid the negative inconsistencies which usually follow problems and cloud your mind. Have faith that the energy *will* change in your direction *if* you change your thinking. Finally, release the problem to the universe and move on in whatever way that means.

CHOOSE YOUR THOUGHTS WISELY

As you move past issues that come about, you may find you're harboring negative thoughts from time to time. Try a simple technique of saying "Stop!" before you even finish the thought. Do this each and every time you find yourself in unconstructive behavior.

All of the undesirable thoughts won't change a real-life situation at all. Negative thinking only produces bad karma. Karma isn't meant to punish you. Its job is to manifest your thoughts and expressions based on the energy you create. Also, negativity permits you, even encourages you, to approach a situation badly. Your subconscious will compose bad feelings deep inside you before you even approach the situation or individual.

Imagine for just a moment…you putting nothing but positive energy into your interactions. Picture you being good, honest, and loving toward others. Modify your attitude to better than that of someone who is pessimistic or negative. Now here's the question. Do you really believe, if you put these positive intentions in place there is a reward for your actions? You might be surprised at the power of intention. If you go into a situation with your mind and heart open to the possibilities, and you consider changing the situation in some positive way, you eventually can change the outcome. People are very likely to flock around you if they see your enthusiasm and optimism; particularly during times of controversy. Wouldn't you be attracted to such a positive person?

So when the next issue comes up say, "Stop!" Then, weigh your options, approach the issue, and proceed productively through the possibilities in front of you. Nasty comments, pessimism, and ultimatums only lead to one party trying to hurt or control the other. Plus, when you take the rights of others by controlling them, they only end up controlling you. Being levelheaded during the process will make a world of difference to the conclusion.

This simple approach works for your thoughts, too. Say, "Stop!" or some other mantra that works for you. Say it three times! You have little to say about a lot in life, but you do control your thoughts.

Those angry, aching thoughts will try to get through, but if you're present, you have the ability to stop them.

Another option is to consider your standards and expectations list to determine the outcome you desire. We will talk more about that later in the book. That being said, you have to know what it is you want. Otherwise, how will you know if what you're dealing with is important? A life changing situation may require a change from you or someone else. Then again, if the situation is only a split-second, get-over-it type of issue, (e.g. a friend ignored you at a party, or your mate didn't call you when expected), you might decide to let the problem go. Whatever it is, it's your call. Take a deep breath and make good choices.

LOOKING IN AND SEEING OUT

Everyone undergoes some soul-searching. You aim to find out who you are, what you stand for, and what your existence really means. It's alright to look deep within yourself to find these answers, but you can get stuck there if you're not careful.

If you're anything like me, I love exploring my past. I like learning new facts about my childhood that I never knew before. I enjoy sitting down with my dad or aunt; those who held insights into my life. I have discovered more about my childhood from their stories than any other outside source. They knew what my mom went through, and they saw what my father had to do for all of us. I don't know where my mom and sisters would be if it wasn't for my dad. He saved us from a very different life. I cherish that as part of my heritage. It's also helpful when trying to understand why some aspects of my past worked out as they did. More importantly, I don't get *stuck* there. I learn from the information and move on.

As you move forward, try to not take yourself too seriously. Learn to find a happy medium where you gain insight, but don't lose perspective. You're here to live and love life, to experience setbacks, and examine your strengths and weaknesses. You need to be aware that your existence has profound meaning. Just not at the expense of your purpose.

While life shows you serious or learning moments, it also reminds you to live it while you have a chance. No one is guaranteed anything or any day. Go live it! Have fun with it! Let the future worry about itself. Or, as I like to say, "God's got this."

Obviously, this does not mean to be irresponsible in life. Nor does it mean you should be insensitive in times of concern, pain, or frustration. Being sensitive means you have compassion for others and that you live your life deeply and profoundly.

To broaden this discussion, I've been told that I'm way too sensitive, and in some cases I'd have to agree. Still, I wouldn't trade who I am for the world. I talk openly (sometimes too much) about subject matters. One topic I address is when I'm concerned that what

I said or did was taken wrong. Ugh! That usually gets interpreted as me being worried or too sensitive. I do worry. I get over sensitive, and I'm even insecure at times. However, most of the time I'm simply talking my feelings out, stating facts, or pointing out interesting details. I learn as I go, and I like making notes on what transpired from various conversations.

Still, when you are *too* sensitive, you either get your feelings hurt easily or worry too much. Being *too* sensitive is when your sensitivity and sensibility collide. That's not good for you. For instance, when I worry too much about what I've said to someone, I find my *too sensitive* side. I think it is fine to care about speaking emotions correctly, but there is a limit. I can explain what I meant, and even apologize if necessary, but I have learned to let my worry go once I do. Still, there are some who feel this is being *too* sensitive…and that's okay.

If you ever heard that you are *too* sensitive, consider they may be right. Take a good look at the times when they say this to you. Does your voice fluctuate to the tone of worry or fear, or are you just voicing an opinion. If you are honest with yourself, you know whether or not you have work to do. Maybe you need to pause for a second and say, "Stop!"

Another way to be overly touchy is with teasing. People tend to kid around with each other. That can lead to hurt feelings when dealing with certain subjects or certain people; especially, when it is taken too far. Pay attention to how you joke around and how you react to being teased.

If you find you are worrying hours or days later about whatever you said or did, get over it. If an apology is in order, take care of it; then, get over it. If you're being teased, and the comments are still respectful, stop taking yourself so seriously. Learn to laugh at yourself. It's important to know when your emotions are appropriate. It's equally as important to know when to discard what should be considered unnecessary or unimportant. You have to weigh what's on your mind.

THOSE OLD SAYINGS REALLY DO HAVE MEANING

Have you ever thought about the old sayings? You know, the phrases that are spoken generation after generation, but the meaning is not necessarily realized at the time. *You reap what you sow, food for thought, I knew you'd outgrow him someday,* and *sleep tight, don't let the bed bugs bite.* Ewwwwwww! There are tons of those little tidbits of knowledge I heard growing up. At the time, I really didn't think about the meaning of them...until now.

I think about all of the time I wasted. I wasn't listening to the advice of my parents and grandparents, or giving much thought to some of the old sayings. Now, I see that I could have avoided some of the mistakes I made.

I remember telling my parents that I needed to make my own mistakes. Yes, of course, it is important to learn as you go. Today, however, I'm a big believer in the idea that a person can learn way before a mistake or bad choice is made. I mean, why make mistakes if you don't have to? Isn't much of the knowledge of a blunder already proven through history? Isn't that why schools teach children the history of our people? We are supposed to gain knowledge from past mistakes, so we know what *not* to do. While it's not always an option to learn from someone else's slip-ups, it is one of the best ways to keep from going down the same beaten path.

On a lighter note, it tickles me when I come across one of the old sayings that give me reason to pause. I may have heard it a hundred times before, but now it makes sense. I ponder them much more than I did *back in the day.* Now, I see the answers to many of my questions. And they were right in front of me all along! I simply chose not to listen with intention...*with purpose.*

So, the next time you hear one of those old sayings: *a rolling stone gathers no moss, what goes around comes around, sticks and stones may break my bones...,* or *be careful what you wish for because you just might get it,* think about the true meaning behind the words spoken.

Another theory that comes to mind is the idea that there is more than one meaning to special words. Case in point, *food for thought,* to me, always meant to take what was being said and to think about it. Now, I have decided these words can have an entirely different meaning. For instance:

"FOOD...FOR THOUGHT"

Consider perhaps that you are feeding your thoughts, your mind, with whatever you put in it. If you think negatively, you are probably eating garbage. Not literally, but yes, literally...and mindfully. What you think about, talk about, is the nutrition you put into your thoughts *and* in your body. The energy you produce and pour out into the world...into the universe.

As told by Rhonda Byrne in the 2006 film, The Secret, and as practiced by many life coaches today, *what you put out there becomes your reality.* This is the discovery of the secret laws and principles of the universe. What you think about manifests its way into your life.

Just imagine! Every scary, negative, dreadful thought you have and worry about coming true. Scary, indeed! So as you ponder through your day, especially ones with drama, trauma, and agony, consider the idea that you can make changes in your day. It's simply done by how you approach it.

If you muster up the courage, and I know you can, give positive imaging a try. I know it will make a difference in your day, your tomorrow, and the next day. Obviously, the trials and tribulations aren't going to vanish into thin air, but what you will see are simple changes to what transpires ahead. Perhaps, if you believe enough, huge changes coming your way!

Try it, won't you? Think of one small thing you want out of your life. Let's say, "I want to see orchids in my life." Boom! They will begin to present themselves. Not in that exact moment, of course, (you're no genie in a bottle) but trust me, you will start to see something new transpire in your life. I decided upon *orchids* many years ago, and today they surround me everywhere. It is the reason I named my company, White Orchid Publishing. I've been told the meaning of an orchid is new beginnings, which fits really well with my journey, too.

So what do you want? Do you want a specific vacation, a new job, a certain flower or sweater, or maybe a favorite color? Create a vision board. Make a place to put pictures and words of all the wants and must-haves in your life. For now, come up with one thing you want to see happen. Name one thing you want to get in your life. Make it simple, "I want to see _____ in my life."

Another idea on manifestation is to create a list of affirmations. This is where you write down all of the positive endorsements that accommodate your dreams. Simple! Whatever is a negative, state it as a positive. Make "I am sick" into "I am healthy and well," or "I am broke" into "My wealth is constantly increasing." Keep this list handy to constantly remind yourself to *look* for the positive so you can *create* the positive.

As you focus on revealing various effects into your life, many will veto the idea that affirming or visualizing comes from the universe. They will say that if you add a thought to your subconscious that obviously it does come to fruition. I agree to a certain extent. If I want a new job, I'll go look for one. If I want a vacation, I'll book it. That being said, what if this idea of envisioning what you want is true?

What if you decide it is utter nonsense to change your thinking? What if you downplay the idea that you should *expect* good things will just come to you? What if you're wrong! Wouldn't you want to kick yourself for not consciously manifesting sooner? Go ahead; mindfully live your life. Wait to see what reveals itself. Simply stated, think *food…for thought*.

The Secret, www.thesecret.tv
Author of quotes unknown

BREATHE NEW LIFE INTO YOU

Every single day you wake up and determine what you want or need to do on that given day. Perhaps you already have responsibilities or plans for the day. Maybe you are one of the lucky ones who take the opportunity to decide day by day...in the moment.

Either way, while making daily choices, base those decisions on what will make your day go well. Don't choose your attitude based on what you have to do that day, how you feel at the time, or whether you woke up on the right side of the bed. When you decide how your day begins, that determines how it will go for the rest of the day. If you chose a good disposition, the rewards are endless.

Obviously, people have obligations that demand their attention. It's in *how* we handle those responsibilities that matter the most. For instance, what if you have a job that requires you to wake up every day at 6:00 am? You're not a morning person, so you stumble out of bed with a grim look at what the day has in store. You don't want to feel this way, and you know in an hour or so your spirits will perk up, but your head still hangs low for a time. Then again, maybe you love the idea of *early to bed and early to rise* so 6:00 am is the perfect time for you, but the workplace you must go to is less than satisfying. Either situation can make for a lot of hard work to get in a good place; physically, emotionally, mentally, and spiritually. Still, it is possible.

Here's one thought to change the way you look at your day: tomorrow you have the potential to become homeless, helpless, or gone. With those options available tomorrow, wouldn't you want to make the most out of *this* day? It's true, you know. You could be in worse shape by tomorrow. Just take a look at those around you. Even worse, think about those who are now gone from your life because of an unfortunate accident, an irreplaceable action, or a dreadful disease. Look at those who roam the streets, homeless, because the economy pushed them down. These are worthy reasons why you should be grateful...*right* now.

Another option, and the one I say each morning, "Thank you, God, for another day." Try to stay in a bad mood after saying that!

Believe, me, I'm not a morning person, but reminding myself to be grateful for the life I lead is important. All in all, I really can't complain because I am still here.

The beauty of becoming more mindful is not only do you begin to see where you messed up, but you see how to fix it! Yet again, you gain the ability to see the heaviness life has offered others. You get a deeper understanding on why your parents and grandparents said certain expressions. You see why they felt the way they did. Perhaps the depression, war, divorce, death, or other changes in their world made them cynical, or better yet, more spiritual!

And so, as you continue down the path of life, you will find worry, anger, agitation, and disappointment at times. Hitting a 'low point' on occasion is very easy to do. Just look! The world is not the same as it was years ago. People are not the same. Times have changed. Some changes are for the good; some not so good. These are the times when being intentional about how you react becomes your blessing.

Hopefully, with wisdom and experience, you do look back every now and again to see what you missed in the moment. Being able to capture that knowledge can help you or someone else as they move along in life.

"No one ever said life was fair," said parents everywhere to their children who didn't get what they wanted. And although we survived without all of our desires, many of us still haven't discovered how to live like there is no tomorrow.

To add more to the discussion, someone once told me that I needed to learn to care less. Not *care a less*, but *care less*. It took me a long time to understand what that meant. It's about avoiding the temptation to try and control what anyone else decides for *their* life. It has nothing to do with not loving people who care about you. It's about giving up the ideals in your head of what should be. It's about learning to *let go* of what troubles you and start living as the day unfolds.

To be clear, there are a couple of changes that happen with caring less. First, you stop fretting over what isn't working in your life by focusing your efforts elsewhere. Next, if you're not getting what you want in a particular situation or relationship, it generally turns around to greet you, more on your terms. Why? Because it wasn't forced; you stepped back and allowed the moment to unfold. Just like your day.

For those situations or relationships that don't go your way, or that don't greet you on your terms, you learn to stop hurting from the demands your mind places on how it *should* be. With mindfulness, you release and let it go.

So tell yourself each morning: Tomorrow you could become homeless, helpless, or gone. Thank God for another day. Be grateful for what you have; a warm bed, a job, a child in the next room. Whatever you have, be grateful.

Remind yourself, you only have 86,400 seconds in a day. Start your day with high expectations. Tell yourself, "It's going to be a great day!"

Quote: "Early to bed and early to rise…" ~ Benjamin Franklin

TO LIVE AND LOVE WITH INTENTION

It can be a bit peculiar to live and love with intention on an ongoing basis? You may get there some of the time, but habitually you withdrawal from the delicacies of life. These are the moments where you *choose* your vision. You can choose to see beauty in a situation, with beautiful backgrounds, or decide to routinely run through the hours with little thought to your blessings. In the rush of life, it is then that you hope someday you learn to live…in the moment.

> *"If you are depressed, you are living in the past.*
> *If you are anxious, you are living in the future.*
> *If you are at peace, you are living in the present."*
> ~ Lao Tzu

When you *live with intention,* you allow yourself to get much closer to the beautiful opportunities every day. Of course, those glorious times are not accomplished without work. Oh, no! You're not allowed to sit back and merely watch life go by. You have to participate. Each time you choose to genuinely partake, your day gets a little bit brighter.

Without question, all of your interactions won't be a day at the park. Each and every time you *intentionally* pay attention may not create an ecstasy moment, but you will be happier…and more productive. In tune with the world, I like to say. And, at the end of the day, you can go to sleep knowing you gave it your all. You are living as best you know how…in the moment!

For that reason alone, you will have good times and memories; even when they are not the best of times.

2
Face to Face
With You & Your Choices

"Knowing yourself is the beginning of all wisdom."
~ Aristotle

AFTERTHOUGHT

I am a firm advocate for creating a solid foundation by taking a good hard look at myself. I will ponder where I came from and what choices I made through the years. When life isn't going well, I can be sure the answer lies within me.

I also know that everything I believed to be true…wasn't. I had to question some of my beliefs. I held strong to some, while changing others along the way. The world is my stage and I don't have to take every cue given to me.

That's one of the many reasons I write. To give you the opportunity to question what you know. What do you accept as real and what is up for consideration?

I also want you to find your passions. I think it's essential to *know* what makes you the happy human being you aspire to be. While I'm no pro, I love to paint. The brush hitting the canvas gives me a feeling like no other. I am at my most peaceful in those moments. That's what I want for you. I want you to find the spark that keeps your fire lit. That part of life that gives you peace, fulfillment, and contentment. You will *know* when you get to the good stuff.

While you're looking at how to create change in your life, some of the easiest modifications are to give the best of yourself to those you encounter. This is for them *and* you. Sometimes, that means being kind and generous with whatever you have to offer. Other times, bringing your best self means to hold back and allow others to figure it out on their own. To be your best doesn't always mean being agreeable, but to be truthful, first and foremost.

I genuinely believe you can create change in any given situation. That also doesn't mean you get everything you want from each circumstance or relationship. It simply means that by being conscious and intentional about your interactions, you remain true to yourself. You create an outcome that is best for your well-being.

One of the biggest challenges you will face is changing how you perceive what's going on around you. From a different viewpoint, you have more control over your reaction…and possibly the outcome. Your happiness depends greatly on how you look at each part of the big equation. Even more essential, how you decide to react to any given situation.

Through my sharing, my wish is for you to understand why people do what they do. Not to mention, why you do what you do. And if I learned nothing else, I know when you understand yourself better, then, you will figure out the rest.

ANCIENT HINDU STORY

I appreciate this analogy on our reaction to troubles. When you find a way to detach from negative situations, to let go of feelings of extended pain, then, you have grown. Troubles come and go, but how you react to that pain is critical to your health, well-being, and longevity. If you continuously live from a place of pain, you might as well make plans to be sick the rest of your days. You have to find peace from your pain by putting it in perspective, and by holding onto your faith.

How does it taste?

There was an aging Hindu master who was tired of hearing his complaining apprentice.

He handed the apprentice a glass of water and a handful of salt.
He told the apprentice to drink from the glass.
He asked, "How does it taste?"
"It is very salty," said the apprentice.
After that, they took a walk heading toward a lake. He handed the apprentice a handful of salt and told him to put it in the lake. He asked the apprentice to take a drink of water from the lake.
"How does it taste?"
"The water taste clear," said the apprentice.
The master continued with his lesson by explaining…the pain of life is pure salt; no more, no less. The amount of pain in life remains the same, exactly the same, but the amount of bitterness we taste depends on the container we put the pain in. So when you are in pain, the only thing you can do is enlarge your sense of things.
Stop being a glass, become a lake.

Author of story unknown

WHAT THE MEDIA PORTRAYS ABOUT WOMEN

Some statistics for you:

- 53% of thirteen-year-old girls are unhappy with their bodies. That number increases to 78% by age seventeen. (Forbes)
- 65% of women and girls have an eating disorder. (Forbes)
- 17% of teens engage in cutting and self-injurious behavior. (American Psychological Association)
- Rates of depression among girls and women have doubled between 2000 and 2010. (Forbes)

These stats are from a while ago. Can you imagine how much greater the numbers are now! The world is constantly changing into new ideas and movements. Unfortunately, not all of these changes are for our own good.

While I am seeing a little change in advertisements, the media tends to display women who are slender and beautiful. The world likes to look at them, too. From that vantage point, it makes being a woman a lot more difficult than it needs to be. Being *average* becomes unattainable for many of us. This portrayal sets up disappointment where none should be.

There are a lot of women who have to work on improving their confidence level. Yet, the young woman who experiences suffering in some way has even more work to do. Not only does she have to achieve the goal of increasing her self-esteem and awareness, she has to conquer the anguish of whatever she went through in the past.

What the media portrays about women, tells men (and women) what to *expect* from women. Is that fair? Do women hurt themselves by buying into some of what the media says about them? I believe the answer is yes.

As a woman walks her journey, she needs to remind herself that she is unique, special, and smart. She needs to carry herself in that way, too; remaining confident and self-assured.

Men need to know that each woman, big and small, is powerful and full of love and grace…in her own way. She is not what the media or anyone else says about her. It is what *she* says about herself that makes all the difference.

www.apa.org/monitor/2015/07-08/who-self-injures.aspx
www.forbes.com/sites/samanthaettus/2011/10/21/25-alarm-bells-for-women-sounds-from-miss-representation/#4cf4362e6240

KNOW WHAT YOU'RE MADE OF

As I started thinking about who I was and where I came from, here are some of the questions I would ask myself. Consider these questions as you look at your own life:

- ♥ What was I like as a child?
- ♥ Where did I come from? What was my environment as a child?
- ♥ Am I the person I envisioned I would be when I grew up?
- ♥ Am I proud of the person I've become?
- ♥ What rough patches have I been through that alter the way I interact with people?
- ♥ Am I being honest with myself and am I living as a genuine person?
- ♥ Do I live as I always have or have I tweaked my surroundings in drastic and different ways? Are those changes for the better?
- ♥ Do I have any standards or goals? What are they?
- ♥ Do I have a written list of my morals and values or just ideas of what I believe in my mind?

These questions should make it clear that *you* should be your main focus. Start with you and your personal foundation. Just as a house can't be built with small sticks, your persona can't be built on loose or lazy character traits. Once you start creating a good foundation for yourself, the next step is learning how to generate good relationships and handle conflict.

Yes, your goal through this entire process is to first create a good foundation. Know who you are, then build on the skills you need to move forward. Both your groundwork and skill building is imperative to the process. When you do acquire the skills you need, you'll know better how to deal with people and situations that arise.

If you've traveled a few rocky roads along the way, rebuilding your foundation and learning various relationship building skills will help you to remain genuine to yourself. When you go through various struggles along the way, those challenges can alter who you become and how you react to the outside world. Become the type of person whom you like and appreciate. Learning about you is the first step. Are you who you think you are?

The other part of the equation is how others perceive you. When someone else shares with you how they see you, you're given an opportunity to discover other intricacies of your character. Maybe you are unconsciously sending out signals or behaviors you would rather you weren't. Although you don't want to waste valuable time worrying what others think of you, and the old adage that you shouldn't care what people think might be true, their opinion can be very informative when trying to make a change within you. Listen objectively.

Sometimes, you get this information from those you influenced in life. My friend, Patti, told me that her daughter used to say, "I'm just like my mom. I'm made out of steel." After hearing those words, she realized she had given her daughter the same crutch she had used all of her life.

Because Patti's young life was riddled with complications and disappointments, she created a wall that sealed her pain away. Worse yet, she passed that onto her daughter. When she realized what she was teaching her, she got an overdue wake-up call. She cried, apologized to her daughter, and then cried some more.

With this new information, she quickly changed the way she interacted with all of her kids. She saw her own bad habit of playing the tough girl in situations. Those times when she thought she was being strong. She finally understood there was a difference between the two. While she thought she was being powerful, she was actually exhibiting weakness.

Being strong requires self-control, self-awareness, and the ability to stand up for yourself. Demonstrating strength means you find ways to respect other people's opinions and characters, while standing your ground. Being a tough girl, on the other hand, generally comes with a rough exterior, a hard core mentality, and a withholding of emotions. This can be debilitating in relationships. Being tough is just another way to hide how you truly feel.

Strength gives you the ability to handle most occurrences with dignity and respect. Strength leaves you with pride and integrity. Strength does not portray arrogance or sarcasm because there's no need for either. Toughness generally leaves you in a vulnerable state, feeling emotionally drained or stressed. When you're strong, you know you handled the situation in the right way…and with the right words.

During the next year or two, Patti learned how to make love flow in her relationships. She figured out how to love in the *correct* way. She had shown her kids a lot of love, but she also illustrated a tough exterior to them. She wasn't made of steel. She was passionate, vulnerable, loving, and kind. Her problem was that her past had gotten in the way.

After getting in touch with her spiritual side, Patti's relationships fell right into place. She attributed that connection to her wake-up call, her learning, and most importantly, her Almighty God. She had to first be genuine with herself and others, along with finding her connection to God. Without this realization, none of that change was possible. She had to believe in herself, be honest with herself, and trust in God in order to find her inner peace.

Once Patti had come to terms with her past, she figured out how to love *with purpose*…in a new and exciting way. She longed to give her children a better example of how to love and live in a kinder way. She wanted them to know there was a better way to be confident and independent, and being tough was not the way for her to go about it.

ROLES PEOPLE PLAY: ADJUSTING BEHAVIORS

How do you think you will be remembered? Will you be known as a hard worker, a quiet contender, or an opinionated and demanding person? Will you be thought of as an optimist, or a tender, loving person? Will you be portrayed as a taker or a giver in life? Will you have had a balance of each of these elements?

As you get older, you may discover you're more like your parents than you ever wanted to admit. Figuring out what you carry with you can be quite humorous at times. Especially, since you probably said you'd never say or do some of what you now find yourself saying and doing. On the other hand, you don't have to carry on any unwanted features of your past. You have the ability to make the necessary changes in your personality and character as you go.

With consideration of the fact that you were mainly educated with what you know through your family and surroundings, still, it's up to you to surpass that history. Live up to a greater potential. If you are acting in a way that doesn't speak well of you, try stepping out of past-created behaviors…so you live your best life. Everyone has past experiences they may not be proud of, but you have the skill to stand out and be counted for all you're worth. Let go of your learned behaviors and responses. Form new, healthier ones. Be able to tap into your full potential. In other words, don't believe everything you think you know. Consider other options.

If what society says is true, and women can do whatever they want, then what is stopping us? In most cases, you can be whoever you want to be. You do this by showing up for you…first. You don't have to play all of your roles out of some sort of obligation. You can choose to just be you!

That's especially true when the roles don't suit you. Some roles you should leave behind. For instance, just because you make a sales pitch at work, that doesn't mean you should keep selling yourself once you're in a personal setting. And just because you have been disciplining children all day, doesn't mean you should reprimand your mate when you get home. Actually, the fewer roles you find yourself playing, the better you'll be for you and those who love you.

Obviously, some roles are necessary. If you are a mother, you inevitably play the roles of disciplinarian, role model, and caregiver. When you're at work, you have to show professionalism and a good work ethic. If you're not careful, you can spend all of your time in some of those necessary roles; in that, losing your true identity. When you continually stay in your roles, you stop living genuinely.

In order to stay balanced, take time to connect back to your true self. Imagine for a moment the actor who never walks away from the part he plays on a set. However, now, he is reacting to a personal situation. Or how about the psychiatrist who is always evaluating patients, and continues to do so while talking to a neighbor or friend? Then, there is the English teacher who corrects the grammar of others while having conversations outside of school. In each instance, the unique person gets lost inside their role.

Look at your life for samples of how you or others might hold onto roles. Do you know a mother who anxiously watches over her adult children, long after they should be on their own? Do you know a professional who takes their work home every night; giving up the time spent with family?

Know when it's time to separate from your roles and just be yourself. One way to stop role-playing is by *choosing* not to ask questions. You don't have conversations or take calls that are not suitable to your balance.

For example, a mother who worries too much should stop asking questions about matters, such as financial concerns, when they are already being handled by her adult child. If she doesn't ask, the responsibility remains with the person it belongs to. The assignment of worry is then discontinued. You wish well for your child and give it to God. Another case is the overworked professional who should commit to cutting off all discussions and phone calls at a certain time. Then, he or she can spend quality time with the family.

When you have an issue with your roles disrupting the balance, putting boundaries in place can alleviate problems. You also enhance the quality time in your personal relationships because you made them a priority. Still, men and women are very different in how they perceive situations, responsibilities, and values. Men tend to enjoy playing certain roles, such as the provider and protector. Women tend to put their priorities toward being caregivers and nurturers. Of course, not all people are the same, but many of us do hold these particular traits. The key, still, is to know when to take off certain hats.

Maybe, for a change, you need to look out for you instead of everyone else. Perhaps, your mate could show more love toward you. Then again, it could be time for you to put work away or turn off the television set. Whatever is getting in the way of your best self, make the change. Become aware of the present moment…so you don't get lost.

Remain sharp and attentive to whether you are role-playing or being genuine. If you're able to do that, you'll know when your relationships are full. Despite your eccentricities, your self-esteem and confidence level will be healthy and strong because you're complete. All you have to do is be yourself. Then, your love and your life will be based on truth.

ALWAYS BEING NICE

Women tend to always do things they don't want to do because they don't want to seem unkind. They want to be labeled as being nice.

Some women take harsh comments from others. Then, there are those who have orders spewed at them that are less than satisfactory. And still others who receive treatment from their partners that is way below their standards. Then, without question, they find a way to get back to a place of peace by being nice. When will women stop reacting in such an agreeable way? How do we stop what society has placed upon women?

When a man is assertive in conversation they are showing leadership. When they behave in a way that is unflattering or boisterous, the behavior is dismissed as being normal. If men don't show up for an event or appointment, they are considered busy. It is accepted without judgment. Or it's let go because, after all, they are men. Women, on the other hand, are judged as being bitchy, nasty, or obnoxious. They are given the labels of unfriendly, rude, or not true friends when we miss an invite. Why is that?

Women were brought up to always be nice. As the saying goes, "Sugar and spice and everything nice; that's what little girls are made of." Sound familiar? This rhyme has been around since the eighteen-hundreds and is still spoken at times today. Of course it's always nice to be nice. All of us should try to show a little more kindness these days. Still, you don't have to take treatment that is less than fair in the interim.

It has always been considered unruly to make waves or get out of control as little girls. Boys were *expected* to be a little more wild and extreme (frogs and snails and puppy dog tails…). This, in turn, created a lot of women without a voice. When you look at all the criteria for being a woman it's no wonder we get a little frustrated. How can you be yourself, if you are always trying to fit the mold you were told was you?

When you give yourself permission, without guilt, to speak your mind and stand up for yourself, then, you will begin to lead a fuller life. You start to understand how freeing it is to do what you think is best, for you, when controversy arises.

Let's say you wanted your steak medium rare and it shows up well-done. Why should you be expected to eat it when you are paying for the meal? Or, you have a great idea at the monthly coworker meeting and you're full of passion to share it. Only to find you're afraid what others might think of you so you keep quiet. Or you need a little down time because you've worked sixty hours this week, and you just don't have it in you to make that invite on Sunday afternoon. Will the world stop? No, it will not.

Asking for what you want doesn't have to be a battle. It's doesn't mean you are mean. You don't have to be nasty in your request. You only need to be assertive. Kindness is still a factor and can be generated in these types of situations.

Take this example of mine.

Years ago, I went on a date with someone I had been seeing for a month or two. With time, I realized he was combative in nature. I started to figure that out because everything had to turn into a discussion. He was handsome, kind, and showed gentleman qualities, but he enjoyed a good debate.

One time, we went to dinner at a nearby restaurant. It was busy so we had to sit quite a distance from the service area. The waitress came over and asked if we needed a refill on our drinks. He said yes and I said no. By the time she came back with his drink, I realized I actually *did* need a refill. I said, "I'm sorry but I do need another drink." She assured me she was fine with it and went on her way. It was in that moment, I knew there was a problem.

My date said, "Why are you apologizing? That is her job."

I replied, "She went out of her way for me, and I wanted to apologize for not asking the first time she came over."

This became the conversation for the next ten minutes.

What is the big deal about apologizing to someone who goes out of their way for you? I used to serve customers in the past and understood how it could be a tad annoying when a group made intermittent requests; sending me back and forth multiple times.

Personally, I see absolutely nothing wrong with showing a little thoughtfulness to someone. I still asked for what I wanted. I got what I wanted. And I did it with consideration of her service. I was being nice *and* assertive.

It was then that I realized I didn't need to stay involved with someone who had issues with such a simple thing. He lost both ways. He didn't like that I wouldn't argue the point. Soon after, he lost me. He was a good guy; but different from me.

In this story, and many other scenarios, there is a way to be nice *and* assertive. You don't have to show anger or use harsh words. And you don't need to stoop to another person's judgement on how things *should* be. Basically, you only need to get your point across in a respectful way.

Some women make a habit of feeling guilty when they stand up for themselves. They will beat themselves up for whatever they said, did, or didn't do for quite some time after an event. That needs to end.

The big lesson here is for you to feel the need to get what you want out of life. No excuses, no explanations. There is no need to feel ashamed or guilty. You're only asking for the same consideration everyone else wants. To live a life that works for you!

Life will change the day you allow yourself to give *to you* without the feelings of guilt. Send that steak back, decline that invitation, or stand up for what you want and need. There is no reason to see yourself as mean, hateful, or any other negative innuendo. You are here to be of service and do kind gestures for others, but in ways that work for your life. Simply put, you have to think of you, too.

It may feel awkward at first, for them *and* you. Soon, you will see the situation for what it is; you standing up for yourself. Once you see how easy it is to hold your position, you'll look forward to the next time you have the opportunity to give to yourself. Free of guilt or shame. It truly is empowering.

https://en.wikipedia.org/wiki/What_Are_Little_Boys_Made_Of%3F#Lyrics
Author of quotes unknown

TELL IT LIKE IT IS

I've been told I am overly assertive or that I *tell it like it is*, and that is true at times. Words pop out of my mouth before I even have time to shut my trap. I always thought this was my strong suit. I told myself that the words I spoke were acceptable because I provided honesty. It's true I was being honest, but how did I come across to others? As my husband told me on one of our very first dates, "You don't sugarcoat it."

Since I was already in the process of becoming more self-aware, I thought this was a good time to incorporate what I was being told. I realized I had some character flaws. Imagine that! I came to this conclusion after many conversations with my spouse, my boss, and some of my friends.

I never spent much time thinking about what I was going to say. I just blurted out what I thought were clear or deep feelings, only to find that I was speaking my mind without consideration. It wasn't that I wanted to be cruel to anyone, I just didn't think before I spoke. No one wants to go through life being misunderstood. I know I didn't.

Another *ah-ha* moment came from long ago. My past had made me less than open with my feelings. At the same time, my past gave me more than enough to say. At times, when I was involved in a conflicting situation, I would react, speaking quickly and without thought. I would try to protect myself with less than happy words. Sometimes, I tried to make a point with these ill-spoken words as a way of speaking up for myself, but not with the truth I wished I could speak. Often times, the words were not my true feelings. I was left with much regret for saying too much. I was playing the role of being tough.

An example of this might be when you are mad at someone. You become sarcastic and think you're being playful, but the words you speak are harsher than you realize. All you really want is for them to show you they care. Since you don't have the courage to express your feelings, you lash out instead with insensitive comments.

If your relationships aren't working well for you, maybe it's time to take a look at changing them. I thought I was assertive, but now see I was being aggressive and tough in some of my conversations. I wasn't intentionally trying to hurt anyone with my words, but sometimes my opinion or feelings weren't expressed correctly. This was especially true when I was in a vulnerable state.

For instance, if I felt hurt or started to question whether someone had my best interest as their priority, I'd aim for words that were cocky or cynical. I didn't get any joy out of hurting another person, but rather longed for some type of reaction that showed me they cared. Perhaps I wanted to protect myself from more emotional scarring and pain. Still, the end result was the same. I spoke harmful words that were unnecessary and unproductive.

I still have assertive and aggressive opinions at times, but I make a mental note of my mouth before, and sometimes when, I've overstepped my boundaries. If I'm aware that what I said might have been interpreted wrong, I'll revise my statement or apologize to the person…in the moment. In order to correct whatever wrong I've done.

With time and mental presence, I have found that many times whatever topic being discussed really didn't matter to me all that much. Not to mention, my opinion was personal and subjective. Of course, there are important conversations, but what about those that don't personally concern me?

An example of this is when someone has a strong point of view about a current issue going on in the world, but I don't necessarily agree with them. I ask myself if this topic is worth sharing my conflicting outlook. Could I possibly damage or ruin my relationship with this person? Am I better off simply keeping my thoughts to myself? Then again, maybe I'll just give my opinion and not argue it.

If the topic is personal to me or in regards to a topic where I have great convictions, I am probably going to assert my viewpoint. However, I do so with complete awareness. I know there are consequences if we don't respect each other's opinion. More times than not, many of these interactions only brought me more frustration, and my two cents didn't change the outcome anyway.

It took me years to figure out that I created some of my own unhappiness. I cared too much about issues that didn't change my day-to-day living. Now, I realize that if the outcome isn't going to change because of my opinion, then I need to consider if I should even give my thoughts a voice.

Today, I still enjoy good conversation, giving advice, and even having a good debate on certain subject matters. Still, I've established the practice of looking at the outcome *before* asserting myself in conversations that don't carry profound meaning to me. In most instances, I recognize when it's appropriate to stand my ground on certain matters and when to keep my mouth shut.

Consider what is important to stand up for and what isn't worth the fight you are giving to the matter. Think of a time when someone misunderstood what you said. Perhaps your words came out wrong in a conversation. You didn't mean any offense, but you still ended up apologizing for how you presented yourself. Maybe you wrote your note in capital letters, which sounds like shouting to the reader. You just didn't understand the rules of engaging.

Articulating yourself in the wrong way happens to everyone at some point in time. It's easy to do. Stop and think about what you are going to say *before* you say it. This is even truer for the outspoken personality because we tend to say a lot more about everything.

MAKE THE BEST OF YOU

Ponder your past for a minute. When you were a little girl what was the story you told yourself? Did you say, "When I grow up I want to be a...." Did you say you wanted to be a mommy, a nurse, or a flight attendant? How about a doctor, lawyer, or even the president? Did you imagine how many children you would have in your lifetime?

Now, do you see yourself acting out or living any of those dreams today? If I had to guess, you probably are playing some of the roles or living some of those dreams. While replacing other ideas you had with new ones.

With that said, people are products not victims of their environment. An environment consists of the people and places that surround you in life. Think about that for a second. If you see the truth in that, then you can put all of your efforts toward unearthing those healthy relationships that bestow good qualities on your life. Understandably, you can't choose your family, and you can't always choose where you live or work, but you can decide to limit your involvement when it comes to the particulars in your personal life.

In other words, the type of people you choose to share your life with will partially shape who you become. If you hang out with friends who get into trouble, chances are, you will, too. Then again, if you hook up with a romantic mate who constantly brings you flowers and candy, you will probably feel respected and worthy. What if that guy is affectionate, caring, kind, and all the while, strong enough to stand up for himself...and you? Who do you think you would become with a man like that? On the other hand, if you choose to be with someone who degrades your character, hurts you physically, and dismisses your feelings, who do you think you would become?

Staying focused on the dynamics of loyalty, personal truth, and quality of life can be very complex. You probably yearn to have character traits that make you proud. Besides wanting to have integrity, kindness, and loving features, you likely want to be a good mate, parent, listener, lover, and friend. You may long to be the type of person who has a kindred spirit.

Generally, your circumstances, and conscious choices, will give you the ability to make good on your intent to be a kind person. Embracing the opportunities to be a wise decision maker will advance your good nature even further. Just being a genuinely good person is always a great start, and the dividends are priceless when you combine that with making good choices along the way. Try starting there.

Here's another piece of character advice: in order for you to enjoy the special moments that come your way, try to have a sense of humor. At the very least, have an optimistic attitude. Do you have a playful, silly side? If so, life and love will come much easier for you. If you find you are too serious most of the time, then life probably drags you down, along with those you love. Also, it's very easy to make trivial matters into critical ones when you get too serious or continually hash out the details. We've all found ourselves in a negative place at one time or another.

Starting now, I encourage you to be bold and brave enough to look deep inside yourself to determine whether you are more optimistic or pessimistic when dealing with life matters. Reach outside of your comfort zone and into a better you.

You begin by sitting down quietly and taking an assessment of your character. Ask yourself these tough questions:

- ♥ Do you react well to change? Do you get excited, upset, or just go with the flow?
- ♥ Do you have fun when you're out with friends, or do you sit in a corner moping?
- ♥ Do you look at the positive or negative side of situations?
- ♥ How do you handle conflict? Do you get enraged, walk away from the situation, or calmly try to work things out?
- ♥ Would you define yourself as being happy, sad, upset, or angry most of the time?
- ♥ When faced with adversity, do you think before you talk or merely blurt out how you feel?

As you move forward, become more open-minded and notice how you react. That way you can create more happy occasions and less negative ones.

While you're busy getting to your potential, it's important to live life along the way. Perhaps you should take some risks and explore new, uncharted territories. Maybe you need to become more of an optimist or thrill seeker *because* you've spent most of your time on the path of pessimism or living in fear.

If you don't figure out what makes you happy, it's certain the time will be taken away from you. You won't ever get that time back, and you never know what's going to happen tomorrow. Plus, in the future you might not be able to do some of what you wanted to…due to age, ability, money, or time. Ask someone older what they wish for. I imagine most would say they wish they had appreciated the finer times of life. I bet they wished for more time building relationships rather than careers, along with having little care or worry about the shortcomings.

When you're genuinely happy with yourself, there is a tendency to be more playful, tender, lighthearted, and loving. If you believe you're receiving what your heart desires, then you should listen to that inner voice. If you're living with love and laughter, you're doing something right. If you doubt what is coming your way, then look deeper to seek the answers to those hard questions.

Informative reading, such as this book, guides you to ask the questions necessary to create change. Another way to get resolution is by talking with someone close to you. Obviously, you don't want to bombard those you care about with all of your troubles, but you can use them to get an outside perspective on you and your expectations. Maybe you *expect* too much…maybe too little. Perhaps, you need to lighten up and enjoy more of life.

Once you have your answers, start jotting down the *Top 20 Wishes* you want for you and your relationships FROM YOU. I've given you a place here to do just that, or simply create a table on a blank piece of paper. Don't worry about filling up the page right away. Begin by writing down some notes now. Then, add on as you go through the book and throughout your day.

Push yourself toward what matters most to you. There, you'll find happiness and contentment. This will put you well on your way to creating healthier and happier relationships. You will start to pay more attention to what you are doing and what you are giving.

Being aware is a key step to making change happen. You'll be on the lookout for what you *expect* for, and from, yourself. Once you start realizing what you should be giving and getting, you can look for those qualities in your interactions.

Try to see everything with new eyes. When you go out into the world with an open mind and open heart, you can do whatever you want with your life.

TOP 20 WISH LIST

Make a list of the top 20 wishes you want for yourself and your relationships FROM YOU. What is missing today that you *expected* FROM YOU concerning how you treat yourself and other people? What do you give to yourself and your relationships?

Examples: I need to show more patience, appreciation, kindness, understanding, trust, honesty, confidence.

1.		11.	
2.		12.	
3.		13.	
4.		14.	
5.		15.	
6.		16.	
7.		17.	
8.		18.	
9.		19.	
10.		20.	

The Mindful, Intentional YOU

THE CONTROL SWITCH

When I saw how easy it was to control situations by not engaging in whatever outside forces were happening, I felt a little more at ease. I knew I still held a small part of that control switch to my life. Whenever I wanted, I could simply stop the thought process that was dragging me down…in that moment. And through intentionally quieting myself, I became a better person. A more complete, content, and happier version of what I always intended to be.

With that said, I know everything happens for a reason. While I believe you can put a dent in the plan by using the control switch, the results eventually go to whatever God wants for you. The difference you make in the process is all about free will. You decide whether to make the journey more positive or negative; depending on how you react.

For me, intentional thinking can also make dents in the plan. The dent is a more positive thought process, rather than the pessimistic, fear-based thought that comes to mind. You do this by controlling your thoughts.

Being mindful of your thoughts is based on what you already know, not about what you don't know. I find continuously refiling my thoughts into one of three categories is helpful: positive, negative, and simple nonsense. This helps me gain perspective on what I'm doing for my well-being.

The nonsense thoughts consist of made up stories. I'm talking about those thoughts that aren't even true (never happened) and generally make you feel sad, mad, or anxious. Many times, negative thoughts start, and before you know it, you are into nonsense and untruths.

You might be wondering what to do with all of those fantasy thoughts that make you feel all warm and fuzzy. Like the fairy tale that takes you to faraway places, or the visualization of that fancy new car in the garage. Hey! More power to you! Those are wonderful thoughts to think! Just pay mind to where the story goes. Many times your thoughts can go to a negative place before you even know what happened!

Of course, you will have thoughts that make you sad, too. There is no way around that. You still can actively manage your reaction as you grieve the loss of a loved one or any other major tragedy by staying mindful of where the story goes.

What I have accepted through this process is that sometimes I want to stay angry, be sad, or simply just don't care about being mindful. That's okay! I am human. Eventually, I come out of my emotional turmoil; to a place where I am more logical about whatever occurred. Now, God can take over. I am free.

If you consciously *choose* to stay mindful as you move along, you will find the best option to get to the end result. And you will do so without distractions or stepping all over someone else's path.

So here you go, living life. You are creating your atmosphere individually, consciously or unconsciously, and in control or out of control. You are showing up with heart and soul; weaving it all together as you find your way. And you should surely find comfort in the knowledge that God is ultimately in control. You need only remain present.

Yes, the immaculate exception you must give to the wondrous universe. The space that is always awake and alive. You won't ever know everything while here on earth, but your belief in something bigger than you is a positive thought, not a negative. The idea that there is more than this existence should give you pause and pleasure. To know that there is a power working on your behalf, for your own good, should be reassuring to you. As you walk through this world and imagine what beauty lies ahead, stay peaceful and humble. Know God is there for you…if only you ask.

Stay intentional, and faithful, about who you truly are and who you let into your life, too. Stand for what you believe in and what you value. More than any other choice in your box of life tools, being conscious in those choices can keep the journey peaceful, healthy, and happy. The brain is amazing. Don't let it get away from you.

ADDING YOU TO THE PAY LIST

As you walk through the various aspects of your life, do you consciously recognize who you are, and do you know what you want? Or do you sit back and wait to see what happens?

Are you leading your life, or is your life leading you?

There is no question that life has gotten extremely busy for most people. Between your job, responsibilities at home, family, and friends, where's the time for your passion; your personal purpose? Of course, you want to do your best at work, and you want to be supportive of your family and friends, but what about you?

Are you still sitting back, waiting for someone to come into your life? Or do you let someone else's dream take hold and attach itself to you; living their dream instead of your own? Now, is this dream *your* dream? It's easy to do! You enter into a relationship and everyone has to make sacrifices. The question is, how much?

Are you living your dream, or are you living theirs?

People have been making compromises for ages. That's how people get along! Hopefully, if you chose well, many of your goals and passions are very similar. Even so, you need to allocate some time just for you.

When your passion isn't being served, and that part of your purpose isn't coming to fruition, your demeanor can change. You can become bitter, depressed, and disappointed in the outcome. Even if you've switched up your dreams and passions for someone you love, you still deserve a little 'you' time…for whatever makes you feel complete.

As for 'things'…well, you deserve those, too!

This is not to say that you should get every *thing* you want, but allow yourself some niceties! Why? *Because*...you are special. You deserve what your heart, and pocketbook, desires.

Do you want to wait to get what you want out of life...until...or when...or if....the right career, person, situation shows up? Or, do you want to offer yourself some of the luxuries now? You know, the 'bling' of life; such as, nice clothes, new furniture, or special moments? Do you give yourself permission to splurge now...*before* the 401K is fully stocked or *until* Mr. Right presents himself?

People need to really wonder if they should continue to wait before capturing the finer things in life. I know this might sound contradictory from my usual advice, but it's not. I believe in being thrifty, while also giving myself gifts.

I remember feeling those same emotions in the past, when I was single. I never gave myself permission to splurge. In fact, many times I still feel that way out of mere habit...and my thrifty mindset. The difference today is that I do allow that extra purchase. I can buy what isn't a *need* but only a *want*. And I know the problem with waiting is that the day may never come! So what was I waiting for!

Here are my thoughts on the matter:

I wish I would have spent a little more money and time on myself. I don't mean bypassing my bills, but adding myself to the pay list. I *deserved* to take my son on vacation, I didn't have to play it so safe while buying a pair of shoes, and I didn't have to answer to anyone about my choices. They were mine to make!

In my early *thirty-something* years, I remember the day my friend told me that I deserved more than the local discounted thrift store for my clothing. I earned the right to move up in my shopping experience. I needed to increase the standards on my personal wardrobe...because I was worth it.

So, what did I do...I went shopping! I spent way too much money buying clothes I absolutely loved! I allowed myself to splurge on better quality clothing, regardless of my future. Giving to me was unusual, so this moment was memorable. And you know what...I felt awesome! I felt empowered by letting go for a time. And I felt remarkable in my new clothes! Macy's may not be considered a *high-end* store to most, but that shopping spree changed me. Long before this, I should have gone to Macy's, Kohl's, or other *better-quality* stores to splurge on myself every once in a while.

For me, that night of spending gave me clarity about what I've done my entire life. I have discounted myself. By giving myself permission to *let go*, I saw I deserved a pair of pants that had a silky feeling on the legs, or the sheets with a thread count higher than a hundred. I even deserved a bra that fit!

Of course, I didn't change completely. I still love a good bargain! But, now, I can consciously make the choice to splurge on myself when I want to. I am completely aware of when I'm looking for the biggest bang for my buck, and when I'm hesitantly, but ready, to make that exciting new purchase.

Still, habits are what they are. They die hard. This shopping excursion was years ago and I probably got rid of the last of those clothes a few months ago! More to that point, I even had the same living room furniture for eighteen years before deciding it was time to buy new! Why should I...there was nothing wrong with the set I had! And the best news about my old living room set is that I gave it to a mother in need. No tedious toss into the landfill!

I have a hard time getting rid of material items *because* I still have work to do on myself.

There, I said it! I have work to do on myself.

Even with the knowledge that you deserve the best you can afford, I still hold onto the fact that everything has a life span, and you don't toss an item out until it can't be used. That's just the way I roll!

With that said, don't wait to splurge on you! Give yourself permission to add you to the pay list. You never know what the future holds and you can't take it with you. Contemplate your future and enjoy the present...all at the same time.

3
Stand Out Above the Rest

*"If you want others to be happy, practice compassion.
If you want to be happy, practice compassion."*
~ Dalai Lama

AFTERTHOUGHT

I never really gave myself much credit for my accomplishments in life. I didn't boast or ask for kudos much, if at all. That is, except from my parents.

I remember calling my mom at the first sign of a raise or promotion. I loved hearing her smiling voice shouting words of encouragement. Wow! What a feeling she gave me! I always knew there were two people in this world (mom and dad) who shared in my excitement when I did well. Not to mention, they were the ones who were there for me during my disappointments, too; when life wasn't going so well.

With the exception of a babysitter on occasion, I didn't ask for help from anyone. I only sought help when I was literally desperate. You either offered your services or I did without. I was too proud and independent, and I could do this on my own.

Today, I can say that I have accomplished a lot in life. I raised a son, went through hardship for years, gained a ton of knowledge from other personal development and human resource educators, and found my place in the world with my husband, kids, writing, serving others, loving my grandchildren, quality time with friends, essential oils, and painting…just to name a few. I'm not perfect in any of my purpose, I deal with issues like everyone else, and when they come up, I deal with them. Still, I am more content today than ever before.

Now that I've listed some of my deeds, know I cannot take credit for any of it! This is God's work. I do all of this through God and I hope to make him proud.

I also believe *God is always watching* so I think He knows when I have done well and when I've done poorly. If I put an item back where I found it at the store, I think that makes Him happy. When I fend off negative thoughts that cloud what He does for me, or even when I share a teaching point with others, I think He knows.

To boast about what I've done is to forget how I actually completed any of my purpose; through God. He made it all possible for me to give back. I simply need to say, "Thank you, Lord."

To *Stand Out Above the Rest* is to be truthful with yourself about *how* you think about what you accomplish in life. Do you take every opportunity to tell people what you did? Can you catch yourself the next time you want to boast? Sure, everyone enjoys the feeling of accomplishment, but how much is too much? That's what I've learned through the years. I need to look at *why* I am telling my tale. Many times, I get nudged by my awareness to do a self-check.

Do you see what I mean? Many times, boasting is simply ego (Edging God Out) getting in the way. This is not to say you shouldn't strive to do well and serve others. It's to remind you to thank God for what you were able to do…because of Him. Also, how much of the *good* that you do helps others? How much is part of your purpose?

I have good reason why I believe that finding your purpose is important. I think, when you seek out your passion, you found part of your purpose…if only for now. Does it make sense to you that what you *love* to do could be what you are *called* to do? What about the things you are good at doing? Is it probable that your talent is part of your purpose? Personally, I think so. Still, I think God has a lot more for us to do while we're here. Because of that, your purpose can change in a moment; even switching back and forth. Let Him guide you. So how can you tell if you are fulfilling your purpose? When it feels right with your gut, you probably are right where you are supposed to be.

To keep me grounded as I make conscious choices, I remind myself of a tagline I coined, *Guts & God*. When your gut tells you something, good or bad, listen to it. To ignore it is to ignore the most spiritual place in you.

You probably remember a time when you thought, *something just doesn't feel right*, and you went for it anyway. Then again, maybe you changed your mind because, once again, *something just didn't feel right*. Listen intently to the signs of your body. If you believe God moves you in His way, then listen. He is trying to tell you something. The Universe is trying to speak to you.

WHAT MAKES YOU SO SPECIAL?

Are you a Good Samaritan? Do you take care of everyone else before you ever get to you? You probably have at least one person who gravitates toward you for some assistance. Perhaps they need you as a friend, mentor, or for guidance. Maybe they seek you out for your money, skills, or a bit of your time.

Someone once told me, "We're all on Earth to be used, just not abused." Keeping in mind, *using* is just another way of saying you have a need for another person. And that's okay! Everyone needs human connection, but you shouldn't let anyone take advantage of your kindness or good deeds. Worse yet, allow your heart to be hurt through manipulation, guilt, or shame.

Be a good person, help when you can, but don't forget you. You can't be everything to everyone, and you can't fix all of the issues that crop up. Other people need to lend a hand, too. You can only help and support people in need when your own life is in balance.

When you are able to be of service, options for giving can vary. You might consider volunteering, personal interaction through counseling of others, or by donating money or items. Giving can be accomplished in so many ways for little time or money…and the rewards are often immeasurable. Simply by helping others in your local community, you will start to see more love in your world.

You could make a difference by holding a garage sale or fundraising drive. You can donate all of the proceeds to a needy family, a food bank, or some other organization in your area. Or you could solicit for small donations and bring about one larger donation for one-needed cause. Every kindness you share can help. Even showing up to lend an ear or a helpful hand can provide a person with care or relief.

Every small gesture you make fuels the transformation of your world. According to *The United States Conference of Mayors December 2009 Hunger and Homelessness Survey*, a 27-city sample survey, states that homelessness is on the rise. There are approximately 51,000 homeless persons on an average night sleeping in our city streets. In

2009, the number of requests for food assistance alone increased by an average of twenty-six percent. This is the largest average increase observed in the survey in the last eighteen years. Can you imagine what the statistics are today!

These statistics prove that it's important to lend a hand. And there are many ways to do so. The examples above are only a few suggestions to get you started. Someone somewhere could certainly use some help. Reach into your own heart and determine what form of giving puts a fire in your belly. There you will find the passion needed to succeed in making a difference.

LIVING WELL | LIVING RIGHT

More and more people are talking seriously about how we have the power, and the need, to save our planet by living "greener" for the greater good.

In addition, more companies are choosing recycled material to manufacture their products. The consumer can do their part by dropping off their used items at one of many recycle bins. These days, bins are available just about anywhere. They can surely find one at a nearby store or school.

Other ways to recycle are with hand-me-down clothes. The gently-used items can make their way through a family of multiple children; helping a friend, neighbor, or coworker. At the very least, giving them to a charity and not tossing perfectly good items into the trash.

To help validate my point, I received a bookmark in the mail from St. Joseph's Indian School that I wanted to share with you. On it is printed an ancient Indian proverb:

> *"Treat the Earth well: it was not given to you by your parents, it was loaned to you by your children. We do not inherit the Earth from our ancestors; we borrow it from our children."*

Imagine if every person, in every generation, lived according to this proverb. From the beginning, every child would learn to take care of the Earth and its people. Everyone would learn to give up some of the small, modern conveniences in order to help our children, and our children's children, have a better life. To think, if we could stop being so self-absorbed, we might save a little of our world for the next generation.

Here are a few suggestions that could easily become a habit: place a recycle box under your desk for all of the paper that comes through your mailbox. Or buy a reusable water bottle instead of getting the disposable bottled water from your store. People have water coolers right in their homes these days to combat this effort. This also makes having better tasting water cheaper and easier to manage. Not to mention, drinking from a glass is healthier for you than plastic.

The smallest of gestures can bring about so much change. For instance, if you can't give up your paper plates, why not get plate holders so you use only one plate at a time? Try turning the water off while you brush your teeth. Unplug appliances that aren't in use, and switch over from plastic or foam to refillable cups to make a dent in the future of our planet. You would be amazed at the amount of recycled material that can be collected in a week. Even having a vegetable garden at home can make a big difference.

All of these options may take a bit more of your effort, but the rewards will greet you through the knowledge that you are involved in helping those yet to come. Look at your labor as a positive change in your life; one that helps you *and* others…now *and* in the future.

When you help someone else have a better day, you also benefit by feeling good and being more aware. When you feel good, you relate to your connections better. You feel more self-sufficient and probably a little more worthy of your existence.

Another bonus of working to make a better planet is that your family will probably participate, and then appreciate, that they, too, are helping others. This is a great way to bond with your family. You learn to work together to solve problems, small and large.

KEEPING UP APPEARANCES

The old saying "keeping up appearances" can have several different meanings. As I wrote in section, *Roles People Play: Adjusting Behaviors*, the saying can refer to role-playing. You can get stuck in the parts you're *expected* to play in life; such as being a parent, employee, employer, or spouse. The phrase can also refer to behaving or looking a certain way to maintain the status quo. You could be trying to keep up with the family down the street through materialistic display. Or maybe you're motivated to get a job that requires you to have certain qualities or demeanor. Another meaning is simply you working to keep yourself fit and healthy; to maintain good balance.

How you perceive the phrase determines the quality of the outcome. If you continually conduct yourself in a way that isn't genuine, you may lose yourself in the process. If you're attempting to better yourself, while remaining true to yourself, then, you will find balance.

It's obvious you have to play certain roles as you move through life. Still, aim to be yourself as much as possible during those moments. The best solution is to embody qualities that live up to your morals and values. Be the type of person who is loving, kind, gentle, open, honest, and spiritual.

While you are being your authentic self, there will be times when you consider someone else's needs and desires before your own. Yet, remember *you are only here to be used, not abused*. Use your influence to watch out for your partner's appearance by helping him maintain good health and well-being. Encourage a friend to make good choices and be supportive. Of course, any transformation to better selections is up to them, but you can help by showing you care.

It's important to pay attention to your own physical health, too. Keeping up appearances by maintaining a good balance in health and well-being can make a big difference in your own happiness. If you don't do all you can to care for your body, the results will affect more than your physical outcome. Your mood, health, and attitude can change with how you feel about your physical health.

When you take steps to have healthy teeth and gums, eat right and exercise, you have a healthier vessel to move around in. Or if you take pride in your appearance by taking time to fix your hair, makeup, and clothes, you will feel better about your overall look. That, in turn, picks up your mood.

Consider wearing a flattering dress or silk undergarments for a sexy attitude. You will feel more attractive and exude sexuality. Your attitude will radiate. Make a daily exercise program that lasts at least thirty minutes. Go play catch with the dog, dance around the house, take a walk, or ride a bike. Anything! Some ideas you have to work at while others will just work. Figure out what stands in your way from getting a regimen started and then move beyond it.

Whatever you do to enhance your well-being comes with other benefits, too. Of course, if you're out of shape, you will get in shape. The healthier you eat, the better your body will function. Then, when your physical condition improves, your ability to have more fun and achieve intimacy will increase. Above all, your attitude will begin to change. You'll feel better about yourself, thereby, enhancing how your life is going.

If you haven't got in shape as much as you wanted, know this: self-confidence and being a caring, loving person make up for any lack of physical beauty. This goes for people of all sizes and shapes. If you believe you're lovable, your appearance will reflect it.

If you want more romance or intimacy in your life, start by looking at your own self-esteem. If you have trouble being vulnerable in relationships, practice techniques and phrases that build you up. Here are a few options to consider:

- ♥ Practice positive thinking. Imagine a world where everything is going well and pretty soon at least your attitude will be better. When negative thoughts enter your mind, do your best to push them out by consciously switching what you're thinking about.
- ♥ Have an *attitude of gratitude*. Start thinking about what you do have. Let's say, you don't enjoy the work you're doing. Focus on the fact that at least you have a job. If you are facing issues

within your relationship, remind yourself of the good they bring to your life. Remain grateful for what you do have, while working to improve the less appealing parts of the connection.
- ♥ Give whatever it is that you want. If you want more romance, become more romantic. Many times, people will follow your lead. When you are more attentive toward them, you get more attention.
- ♥ When you are unhappy about something, ask yourself if the issue is worth ruining your day. Put the issue into perspective.
- ♥ Don't run on autopilot while spending your days. Ask yourself what changes you would make if you knew you had limited time, and then go make them happen.

Challenge yourself to create the best mental and physical self that you can. Start with your attitude and grow from there. Invest the time and effort to create your best self.

THE IMPORTANCE OF HONOR

The definition of honor: the concept of a direct relation between one's virtues or "values" and their status within society.

I think honor is what you believe in, the faith you have in yourself, and the integrity you portray in life. Honor helps to create your character. A person with honorable character knows, in their gut, they are doing what is right.

Honor is an *expectation* you place upon yourself. It is what guides you to be the best you can be. A show of integrity that holds true to your beliefs, and stands up for those philosophies when you need to. Honor, to me, means *good people* with substance. Finally, honor is an invisible badge; worn to remind you that *you* are someone who holds true to your word and actions.

> *"Mine honor is my life; both grow in one;*
> *Take honor from me, and my life is done."*
> ~ William Shakespeare

Honor is up for testing at all times. When you think, speak, or act you are being tested. As I tell my grandchildren, "God is always watching." When honor is taken away, regardless if you allowed it or not, it can change your outlook on life and in yourself.

For instance, if someone accuses you of something you didn't do, it can make you angry, sad, or confused. You have various ways of handling the situation, but the accusation is already out there. Your honor and integrity is already being questioned. Another example might be that you weren't as honorable as you should have been in a certain situation. Now, you have to face God with the truth. Can you still live with yourself? God will forgive you, but can you?

Being a person of honor requires good choices during times of difficulty. Many times, the easy way to handle a problem is not the right way. That is why conscious choices are a must; to keep you from making bad choices and becoming dishonorable.

Being honorable means you're not a liar. You have a conscious that knows it's not the right thing to do. You're probably the kindest person in the room, and someone who is always there for your family and friends. Even if you had a hard upbringing, you strive to be honorable. You may not always succeed, but you can admit your shortcomings when necessary. You are humble.

> *"A kind man is known for his generosity and a smart man his wit. A gentleman is known for chivalry, while a man of his word is known for his honor and character."*
>
> ~ K Mitchell

Whatever you're dealing with, and wherever you go, *do* more, *be* more, and *see* more. Know the key is to stay intentional in your thoughts and actions. To *Stand Out Above the Rest*, honorably, means to be or do more (or better) than what is *expected* of you. Sometimes, it means standing up for what you believe in, while other times it's letting go of a conflict that doesn't serve you well. At all times, it's a show of your honorable character in the process.

While you're going through the motions of being honorable in everything you do, remember the only judgment that truly matters is His; your God Almighty. Yes, you want to do right by others, and as part of your purpose, you want to be of service to others. Still, you can try your whole life to please everyone else and it won't add up to much if you fault them in the future. This is why your work must be for God.

You are human and you will make mistakes. You could do everything in your power for someone and in one unfortunate instance it could all be swept away. All of your good could be forgotten, if you have somehow disappointed them. With God, you are always forgiven…if only you ask. The best options are to spend your time and efforts displaying honor, making mindful decisions, and remembering what you do, you do for God.

FORMULA FOR MEDITATION

Discover the secret to *feeling* great while you are *being* great. Stand out by doing what many do not…meditate!

As you continually stay busy, being the best you can be, there needs to be some down time amongst all of the commotion. If you don't, you will begin to wither.

Nothing soothes the body and mind more than meditation. If you would stop and take a few minutes to unwind, you could become more productive, healthier, and happier! Getting all stressed out only adds to the commotion; not to mention, offering us pain, disease, and unhappiness. Aren't those reasons alone enough to get you to carve out just a few minutes for yourself?

Intention, Transcendence, Detachment

Meditation can help create a consciousness within you that changes how you think, feel, behave, and relate; both in public situations and within your own relationships. It can even help with your sleep. Getting your mind quiet *first* can help when you can't get to sleep or wake up with worry.

Life can go in any direction you choose, but only if you believe that you have the mindset and skill for such a mission. Once you have faith in the process of meditation, you will figure out *how* to change direction.

This is not to say you 'flip a switch' and everything is fine, but it is simple logic…*what you feel is real*. Simply change your thought process from any negative thought pattern to one filled with positivity and gratitude. While I believe you are able to maneuver your course in a particular fashion, first, you have to believe you can.

After listening to many spiritual leaders over the years, handling my own personal issues, and taking notes along the way, I learned what you think about, you bring about. And even more impressive… you get to choose!

Of course, God is still my first and favorite, and always will be. In fact, He is a big part of meditation for me. To me, God *is* the Universe. He is everything.

While you meditate, all of life's problems are simply pushed aside for a time. This gives you time to create new behaviors from any past bad ones you normally turn to. For instance, getting upset and boisterous in the midst of a dispute does not work well for conflict. It only angers it! Having no communication is another way you help a relationship to go awry.

As you meditate, all of these thoughts are set aside for a moment. In that, you are given time to appreciate yourself and manage your life with more positive, intuitive outcomes. In time, meditation can teach you *how* to be the best '***you***' that you can be. You become more peaceful, self-assured, and more interconnected with your soul and spirit than ever before.

I created this handout to offer you some simple, yet effective tools to get you started in meditation. My hope for you is more peace.

How to Meditate:
1. Introduce your request; your intention. Ask for what you want and put positive energy toward it.
2. Transcend then into your God space to find inspiration, insight, intuition, gratitude, creativity, and 'thoughtful' choices. These are the "byproducts" of meditation.
God space = God, Higher Power, Universe, Spiritual Guide, Guardian Angel, whatever you want to call it.
3. Detach from whatever it is you want (your request) and let the universe handle the details.

Rules on Meditation:
While I don't believe there are any specific rules to meditation, except to be still, quiet, don't think, and connect with your spiritual side, here are some great tips that may be beneficial to you.

- **Sit or Lie Down?** – Sitting up is most beneficial. If you are feeling sluggish, you may fall asleep if you lie down. On a personal note: while sitting is best for meditation, both meditation and focused breathing works for me on nights when I find myself with worry and can't get to sleep. Try it the next time you go to bed or wake up and struggle getting back to sleep. You can put yourself to sleep in a matter of minutes doing focused breathing and meditation. It's better than counting sheep!
- **How to Sit?** – Honestly, I don't think it matters as long as you feel good. If you're comfortable, your body will give you less noise. You don't want commotion while you are trying to remain calm and quiet. Sit with your legs crossed, pretzel position, or straight out in front of you. I think it's a personal preference. Just be relaxed and open. I would try a few positions to see what works best for you. I change my routine to whatever works for me at the time.
- **Hand Gestures?** – Everyone has a different take on positioning of the hands. You have probably seen where you touch your finger to thumb as a point of connection. While I don't believe positioning is an exact science, each one does have a different meaning or purpose. I suggest you look up the different poses and see what suits you. To help you understand your mission, visualize someone angry and ready to fight; their hands clenched into a fist. Now, imagine trying to meditate in that frame of mind; hands in this tight position. Can you see how you might be less open to receive? The key is to open your mind and body so you transcend into your deeper, soulful, spiritual self.
- **Noise or Quiet?** – You may choose sounds of nature, soft music, white noise, or silence; whichever works best for you. Switch it up. If one doesn't work for you, do something else. I find silence works best for me, but many enjoy the noise.
- **Focus on Breathing?** – You can notice or observe your breath, but don't focus on it. That tends to be a thought. Be careful not to allow your breathing to engage with your mind.

Your breathing will automatically slow down and become deeper on its own. Recognize it happening, but don't *think* about it. While some guides say you shouldn't focus on your breathing, because my mind seems so noisy, I find that paying attention to my breath *first* helps me to transfer into the meditation phase and transcend. I know I need to go deeper than that, so I am not in a thought, but it helps calm me so I can get there faster. I call it pre-transcendence.

- **Mantra or No Mantra?** – Mantras can help keep you focused away from your thoughts. Try mentally saying 'So' on your inhale and 'Hum' on your exhale. Another one is 'Om' which means 'I am.' I learned these mantras from Deepak Chopra as he talked about many variations. Each one has its own meaning. Doing research will help you discover mantras that can guide you toward your destiny.
- **STOP or Ignore Thoughts?** – Don't try to push your thoughts away. Rather, see them fly by and refocus your attention on staying calm. Leave your thoughts alone, and eventually, they will float away on their own. Then, you will transcend. Recognize when you are actually thinking a thought or merely being aware of them. This is also true for visualizing your dreams. Focus on your breath and visualize your dreams *before* meditation. For me, I find that's another portal that gets me to the meditation phase. Just remember, practice makes almost perfect.
- **Where to Meditate?** – Anywhere except when handling dangerous machinery or other critical tasks. You can be in the line at the grocery store or gas station and meditate. If you are on a bus, plane, in your bedroom, or somewhere else… meditate. Anytime you become aware, become quiet, and recognize your inner self, you are in some form of meditation.
- **How Long to Meditate?** – Try to spend fifteen to twenty minutes a day visualizing dreams, focusing on your breathing, and meditating. End your time thinking about what you're grateful for *today*. Continue your search for gratitude

throughout the day; a warm blanket, a hug, the last piece of chocolate cake, or the hand motioning you to come into their lane. Whatever you come across that's a blessing, appreciate it.

Fortunately, the time I spend reminding myself of what I'm grateful for has now turned into my habit. I'm not perfect at it (never will be), but I strive to keep control of my thoughts on a daily basis.

If you spend about twenty minutes a day on meditation and searching for gratitude, that is a good rule of measure. Meditating twice a day is even better! While I don't always reach that standard, I am constantly aiming for it.

> "Trying to silence a thought is a thought.
> The awareness of a thought is not a thought."
> ~ Deepak Chopra

I hope you find these tips helpful as you progress down your life lane. Know you are exactly where you are supposed to be at this very moment. God put you there for a reason. Choose to live your life more spiritually connected to your Higher Power (and you). Then, watch as you soar. I send you all of my best wishes as you continue to learn and grow.

Deepak Chopra: www.chopra.com

4
Conscious Change

*"It isn't always a change of scenery needed to make life better.
Sometimes it simply requires opening your eyes."*
~ *Richelle E. Goodrich*

AFTERTHOUGHT

I truly believe if you aren't ready for change, then change won't occur. That is, of course, with the exception of change that is out of your control. That moment when someone else makes a modification that affects you, and you have little to say about it. Your only choice is to change the way you react to it.

Yes, life will continue to change. Situations will keep happening. Even as you try to control how you react to it, you still have to let go of directing the outcome. Unfortunately, change constantly occurs, it isn't always fun, and many times you won't want to deal with it or accept it. Still, you have no choice. Some things change and there's literally nothing you can do about it. It's that simple.

Luckily, you always retain one aspect of control. That's the way you respond to the new adjustment. Obviously, your thoughtful response requires some effort on your part. Remaining conscious is key to your success and positively worth it in the long run.

The other type of change that enters life is all about you. It's looking differently at life. Sometimes, you see life through rose-colored glasses, while other times with common sense, distance, or abandonment.

Conscious change encompasses all the variations of change I mentioned. For instance, you have to decide you are ready for change in how your life is going. You make the *conscious* decision to stop doing whatever isn't working. At that juncture, you make the commitment to create real change. You put in the work; then, you reap the benefit of your efforts. When you devote yourself to take action in some way, the universe will follow by giving you what you need. Just keep moving forward and watch to see what starts working on your behalf.

So, as you continue making life choices, remember you always have at least two choices in front of you. You will continually run across mistakes you made (or make) when creating those conscious choices. You will either realize you made a bad choice in the moment, or see that you didn't stay conscious and intentional during an interaction or situation. Don't beat yourself up as *that* is merely part of the new thinking process, and another way your mind tries to control you. Just keep thinking *conscious choices*.

Here, I share with you the exact moment I knew I was ready for change. Real change! And the challenges that came with that decision.

ARE YOU READY FOR CHANGE?

There comes a day when you say to yourself, "I'm ready for a change." You're ready to take matters into your own hands and make them work for you. Maybe you want to curtail certain aspects of your life. Be it a relationship, a career, or some other important piece that needs adjustment. Perhaps, the change you want to see needs to happen within you.

I remember the day I knew I was ready for change. The day was like any other day. I had a great job with a well-known corporation. My salary was increasing steadily, and life was going extremely well for me. The people I encountered in the workplace were kind, friendly, helpful, and smart. Each day I learned something new, and I was excited to be in an environment that continually challenged me. I had a beautiful home, a new car, and family and friends who I loved with all of my heart. Unfortunately, there was still a piece missing in my life.

Everyone's personal life is in need of adjustment every now and then. You may enjoy the people in your life, and have a lot to be thankful for, but still long to share some of your time and love with someone special.

My personal life was in need of adjustment, too. I really enjoyed having my loved ones around me, and I had a lot to be thankful for in life. Still, I needed to fill the void that had been present for so long. I was in a great place with my friends and family, and was becoming successful in my chosen career. In short, I was feeling good about my future. Still, after twenty years of dating, I had a spot that needed to be filled. I knew something was missing. I sought more substantial meaning in my life and I was ready to get it.

It was around this time that a coworker of mine told me about a week-long seminar he had participated in. The class was based on personal development, which was exactly what I needed at the time. He told me the experience had changed his life. He spent a lot of time sharing his story with me. He explained how his self-confidence had increased, his goals were more in focus, and his communication skills were greatly enhanced. He said a lot of people working in the company had already attended the event. They had started a network, which allowed them to continually share and support each other. After listening to his story, along with hearing how so many others were impacted by this event, I knew change was possible.

I realized I was at a standstill on my path. I had the will to move forward, but didn't know how to proceed. After long discussions with my coworker, I found there was a different way to look at my situation. There was another way to consider why my life felt as if it were on hold.

I announced right then and there, I was ready to make change happen in the way I lived my life. I could actually *feel* the adrenalin pumping through me at that very moment. I knew I was ready. I knew it was up to me to take a proactive approach and make big adjustments in my life. He gave me the information and off I went.

I can honestly say that this was where I stepped onto a new path. I'd still make mistakes, but my growing process was underway, and I was excited to get started.

On the first day of the seminar, I walked into a large room; very scared and alone. The room was filled with other lost souls wanting to understand themselves better. Almost immediately, one by one, the group started sharing with each other. That put me at ease quite a bit. I knew I was in the right place…at the right time. I was ready to open myself up to change and my journey was about to begin.

I quickly discovered how to see the world through my mother's eyes; instead of mine. I did this simply by listening to another woman talk about her situation. By the second and third day, I learned how to forgive certain people who had hurt me the most in life. One of whom was me. I understood how to connect with my inner child through meditation. I rapidly learned to openly communicate with others. Most importantly, I knew where to look for the pain I held onto so tightly. I was amazed to realize that some of the issues I thought certain were over, were the very ones holding me back.

One of the last exercises was to get feedback from team members about what they thought was my biggest challenge. One by one, the group shared their thoughts with me. The opinion was unanimous! I needed to stop beating myself up! They told me to put the big stick down and give myself a break. I was startled by the fact that now, at the end of the seminar, I was still learning about myself!

I met a lot of kind and interesting people at this event. Some of the people who attended the seminar would grow and some would falter; this I knew. Without a doubt everyone sharing in the experience was supportive of each other in their quest for a new beginning.

By the end of the seminar, I had gathered more information than I ever thought possible about myself. Plus, I felt free from some of the baggage I had carried around for years. I gained new strength and power. I was ready to incorporate all of that into my daily life. Not only did I learn a great deal about myself in the process, I realized quite a bit about the people I loved.

During this whole adventure, issues cropped up that I wasn't even aware of until then. That gave me the opportunity to work on those areas, along with creating a new start for myself. I dismissed a lot of my guilt and shame, forgave those who had wronged me, and opened my heart to receive whatever was coming my way. Change didn't happen overnight, and I still had a lot of growing to do, but I finally had a place to start.

Still, the biggest lesson for me was figuring out what held me back from growing personally. I discovered my past was the culprit. Sound familiar? Unfortunately, many people hold onto their past without ever realizing it is what keeps them from growing into who they are supposed to be. It was then that I chose to address my own.

When I was younger I had experienced abuse. I sustained verbal, emotional, mental, physical, and sexual abuse in one form or another from my teenage years through adulthood. There was even a time as a small child that I had blocked out. This is when an older man sexually exposed himself to me. Luckily, I ran out and went straight to my grandmother's apartment; never breathing a word to anyone.

I have no desire or need to go into all the details of these events. I have finally found my way past those anguishing days. Still, for the purpose of this story, I thought I needed to share with you, the reader, the fact that these harmful acts occurred.

This book isn't about telling the sad story of what happened to me, but rather to share any information I believe can help you avoid regrets. The biggest lesson, for me, was having the right outlook. If I had put the right attitude out there from the beginning, abuse would probably never have come to me. And if it did, I would have been strong enough to walk away from it.

During those *ah-ha* moments of reliving my past, I realized that just because I walked away from the abuse, that didn't mean I was free and clear. I had to figure out how to get past the incidents that happened to me so I could move forward. I needed to forgive myself and those who hurt me.

For years, I walked around feeling so proud of myself because I had gotten out of a bad situation. Truthfully, I wasn't past those issues at all. I had been carrying the pain and anger inside me forever! As strong and confident as I thought I was, these issues were the very reasons I wasn't growing. My strong, confident demeanor was actually a false role. I was playing it tough and proud. Now, I was shocked to realize…I was a fake.

I bring all of this up to help anyone wanting a better relationship. In order to be ready for this enhancement, *you* have to be ready for change. Ready to change the way you see yourself, in the way you are treated by others, and in how you treat them!

Regardless if the revamp you crave refers to a friend, family member, partner, or coworker, you call the shots in your life. If it's change you want in your attitude, job, home, or education, you call it. You need to be your own best friend by standing up for the challenge. Change will always be present in one form or another and the ability to transform with it is crucial.

If life isn't working as well as it should, it's up to you to rectify it. As you spend some of your valuable time making revisions, figure out where you are now, where you want to go in the future, and who you want to take with you on your journey. When you get to the point where you wonder how you stumbled so far off the path from where you thought you'd be, that's usually the time you are ready for change to occur.

Now that you are impelled to make improvements, get excited to experience change within you. At the same time, see the change happening around you. Take your time…it's a process.

Once you recognize your own need for change, you begin to observe the world as a whole entity…undivided from you. You start to realize you have an impact on every situation you are in.

To better explain this thought process, take a look at this scenario:

- ♥ You're having a conversation with someone.
- ♥ Imagine for a minute stepping out of your own body.
- ♥ Now, see yourself stepping into the other person's body.
- ♥ Consider how this person sees you, from their viewpoint.
- ♥ Focus on what they might be thinking about you; right at that very moment.
- ♥ Look through their eyes, at yourself; your behavior, words, and actions.
- ♥ Do you like who you see? Do they like who they see?
- ♥ With this new knowledge, would you change anything about how you're interacting with them?

You're the only one responsible for you. As you go through each day, witness your own thoughts, behaviors, and actions. If you need to stand strong, make sure you're doing so with respect and kindness. Always look for the good inside yourself. Give that part of you to others. That's especially true during times of controversy. Being able to see yourself as part of the world allows you to recognize who you really are.

CHANGING CONDITIONS

Everywhere you go people talk about the current issues that are happening at home and around the globe. You also encounter more people who aren't as friendly to others as they once were. Yes, the world is changing. Times today have become more disruptive than ever, but luckily, you still have the capability to change your own life for the better.

Think about how old you were five or ten years ago, and how the world was then compared to now. Think about how much you have changed in that same time period. Ponder these thoughts for a minute.

It has been said, you have to watch your own back because you never know who's going to hurt you in some way. There are more hate crimes being committed, deadly violence and destruction on the rise, and millions more people homeless and hungry on the streets. You need to find ways to make your world a safer and more loving place to live. For starters, you can decide to look for your particular purpose *and* how you are reacting to the negativity.

Have you ever heard *what goes around comes around* and do you believe in what is called karma? For many, karma plays a major part in a person's religious beliefs and spiritual guidance. Karma is based on the idea that the beneficial or harmful actions and thoughts you engage in (past, present, or future) will return to you in some way.

For example, the generosity or greed of the wealthy man who has whatever it is he wants. He can either help or dismiss the middle or lower class man who is struggling to get by. Someday, he will pay the price for his actions…good or bad. Or the honesty or dishonesty of the woman who makes a choice at the local department store. She either refrains or takes what is not her property. She, too, will see the result of her behavior in one way or another. If you say harsh, callous words to someone, behave inappropriately, or get careless with someone else's feelings, don't be surprised when you're on the receiving end of similar words or actions.

I learned this lesson, in a positive way, at one of my jobs. I was working as a technical advisor. My very first customer had questions about her website. Since I was new to technology, and wasn't at all familiar with her particular software, the interaction could have gone a number of ways.

I remember specifically staying aware of how I was handling myself. I didn't want to express any frustration for my lack of knowledge of the software. Patience does not always come easy to me so I was grateful for my newfound knowledge of being conscious. Eventually, I was able to help her with her website. Plus, I got a new technical tool in the process. Since I was able to help her, she knew I had ability.

Two years later, I was told my technical position was being eliminated. I could either find another job within the company or take the severance package being offered. Since I loved where I worked, I started searching right away for the next position. You'll never guess who my first interview was with; my very first customer. She was the direct manager for this new position…and she hired me!

This was the day I knew it was true. Whenever possible, you should never burn bridges. You don't know how someone might fit into your life later. While you won't hold onto every relationship and connection, just to see where it goes, you can influence results. You only need to do your part in order for the bridge to remain standing. That is, striving for pleasant exchanges and peaceful circumstances.

If I would have reacted negatively in our first meeting, I doubt I would have gotten the job. I needed to be careful how I treated people. One never knows who they will answer to in the future; personally and professionally.

The lesson about faith and mindfulness is clear to me. Instead of feeling emotional or resentful, I could be thankful for the loss of my past job. If I hadn't been put in the position of unemployment, the opportunity for a better profession would have passed me by.

Speaking of karma, have you noticed a lot of people aren't as considerate as they used to be? At times, you run into someone who just isn't civil to you. Sometimes, that bad attitude can rub off on you! With that said, have you ever considered how you are with other people? Are you so wrapped up in your own details that you are behaving in some ill-mannered way? Or, better yet, are you reaching out to create real change? Are you being kind to others?

These deliberate considerations work in every relationship you are in. Many times, you create a different outcome simply by giving a different response. When you pay close attention for opportunities to react in a positive manner, your eyes open to many new possibilities. Remind yourself to be thoughtful when relating to other people. On a regular basis, you need to recognize the spirit in all of your interactions and how you're relating to them. You are in control.

If you change yourself for the better, the impression you make is substantial for you *and* the people you encounter. If a lot of people are encouraged to do the same, to create change within them, it could have a major impact on the world…one person at a time.

Imagine, within a short period of time, the transformations that have occurred in our educational system, our technology, and in the governing of our nation. Even our home and job markets keep changing; one day plummeting and the next rising rapidly.

Now, think even further about how the world has altered in that same time frame. There are more conversations about global warming, energy efficiency standards, and recycling. You hear stories about children and young people being sold as slaves for money, labor, and pleasure. That is, human trafficking. There is more news about child predators, conspiracies, wars, and other harsh realities across the globe. Can you see how changing you, for the better, would only help?

The way people care and nurture each other now faces a new challenge, too. Only a couple generations ago, reaching out to help one another was a way of life. Now, because many in our society seem to look out mainly for *number one*, you have to pay more attention to what *you* are doing. Only then can you sleep better at night, knowing you are doing your part to repair humanity and the mutual consideration that has been lost.

I think most people are beginning to realize that change has to happen. What if people actually did make a shift? What if they could create a kinder, gentler place with more understanding for each other? It would be wonderful to watch the modifications unfold! As said before, putting positive notions out to those we come across can alter the world…one person at a time.

When you figure out that you don't have problems half as bad as someone else, then it's your job to figure out what *you* can do to make matters better. You can help within in your little world or in the vast space of the universe. Whether you carry out a small deed or a big one, creating positive change for others is the best way to start making changes in you. Even taking the time to lend a smile or a *Hello, how are you?* to someone you pass on the street are simple ways to help change the future for the better.

One way I make sure to do good deeds is through a reminder on my phone. Every day my phone throws up a message, "Do a good deed for someone every day." If I haven't done something that day, I reach out to see what I can do. The effort could be as small as making a phone call to someone to see if they need anything. Then again, I could go to the food pantry and put some time in serving others. Regardless of what I do, I want to make myself accountable with a daily reminder.

You'll notice that with each positive adjustment you make in your behavior and actions, the universe will respond to you through kind acts and energies from the people around you. Maybe the change will be as modest as the beauty you see in the world…in that moment. You'll realize that you do have the ability to create a new life for yourself and those around you. Just by changing how you relate with people and your environment.

To simplify the message, stay attentive to what is happening around you. Pay mind to the *Golden Rule* which tells you, "Do unto others as you would have them do unto you." Then, start to modify how you interact with people. Create new bonds by showing kindness to others. Build good karma for your life. And finally, establish a new approach for how you see the world.

Author of quote unknown

STANDARDS | EXPECTATIONS | GOALS

People talk about having standards, expectations, and goals for themselves. When you go to define these characteristics, you'll find there is a difference between the three items. While they may seem similar to you, they are actually quite unique in their meaning. The objective, for you, is to understand what each attribute means to you, and how to apply it to your life. At the end of this section, there is a chart for you to complete. Review the examples listed to help you understand the difference between standards, expectations, and goals. Open your thoughts to what could be incorporated into your own chart.

Standards

Standards are the minimum criteria you set for yourself and your rule of measure for quality, quantity, and value. Standards are the very least you want out of yourself and your relationships. Maintaining those levels are pertinent to your success and happiness. Standards can be modified as your life changes, but they should never be lowered. If you find you are in a situation that doesn't live up to them, in most cases, the situation (or your mindset) needs to change in order to live up to those standards.

Standards consist of boundaries that you were either raised by or ones you placed upon your life, as part of your overall plan. They are the personal, healthy limits you have for yourself, and for other people; emotionally, physically, and spiritually. Generally, if someone crosses a standard you've put in place, you'll have an issue with the intrusion. Hopefully, this gets expressed constructively…so they know when they have violated one.

If you were building a house, would you start without a blueprint? If you were asked to a formal dance, would you show up in jeans? Or, would you go buy the perfect dress? It's foolish to move forward on any significant project or event without first carefully planning the details. Still, you might be surprised that so many relationships, intended to last a lifetime, end in disaster because of a lack of planning. Having a detailed plan of your wants, needs, and desires will help you stay focused.

To add even more thought, laws have been put in place because societies need discipline and standards for how we live and act. A criminal who breaks the law is breaking a social standard. If you're set to go to college in California and have every intention of living there, then hooking up with someone across the country wouldn't be wise. That is, unless you are willing to continue in a long distance relationship or move. As part of your plan, this could become a standard, "Okay, anyone I date has to live in California or wants to in the future."

For those of you who feel children are critical to your happiness, you must discuss the topic of children with your partner. It isn't wise for you to coax your mate into having children, if he doesn't see them in his future. If you don't want any children, but you're involved with someone who does, then marrying him isn't wise either. Unless, of course, one of you plans on changing what you want. This also serves as a concern for those of you who date someone who already has children. Be consistent with your desires, or make a conscious choice to alter your standards. Whatever you choose, either way, you have to live with your choices.

It is fine to make changes to your standards, as long as you're moving forward while you're making these adjustments. When you live and behave below your standards, you threaten your principles and morals. When you choose below your standards, you receive less than what you anticipated for yourself today…as you see it. Of course, there are some standards that should never change, (e.g. no abuse in your life), and others that can be altered, (e.g. an unexpected stepchild, career change, or material item). Whatever you decide, you live with the choice.

During this process, I offer less advice and more examples. I do this because I want you to capture where you see yourself today. You can add, delete, and even change your chart as you move forward, but you have to know where you are today in order to observe the changes you make. Make several copies of the form to make it easier to update it as you move along.

Expectations

Just as important as standards are *expectations*. Expectations are your opportunities waiting to happen. They are tidbits of happiness you want from yourself and others. You can live without these distinct characteristics, but you have the potential and hope of getting them. If you are fortunate enough, you and others will exceed your expectations.

You can raise a child from birth to eighteen, instilling your morals and values as their standards, and *expect* them to become productive, successful adults, but ultimately that will be up to the child. You set the bar high in hopes they rise to meet your expectations, but that is still no guarantee.

Another example of an expectation is that your standard states the mate you marry will have no children of his own and never have been married. Yet, let's say you meet someone who is divorced with a child. You *expected* to start fresh with a mate, but you have fallen in love with *this* man. Your standards, and what you *expected* for your future, may need to change. This is an entry into your Expectation column; something that differs from your standard. If you see yourself marrying this man, you're probably willing to tweak your standards because he meets much of the other criteria you've set. Sometimes, when you have a result that doesn't match up with your standards or expectations it can be okay, and even good, to make the switch. Revisit your list for clarity of importance and desire.

Goals

Goals are the achievements and direction you set for your future. They tend to be more specific than expectations and aim for the perfect ending. Goals are where you direct your intentions. You have the finish line in view down the road. You may not achieve every goal, but you begin with the anticipation of getting what you stated. If you complete your list of goals, the likelihood of you attaining these aspirations is higher. You have a clearer path showing you where to go. Not to mention, a written affirmation directing your steps.

Goals are your ambition toward future events. They're obtained by directing your attention, focusing on certain places, before you arrive there. Perhaps you have a goal to attend a college or achieve the career of producer, veterinarian, or lawyer. Only you know your dreams. Maybe you see yourself married for fifty years with five children; then again, never married at all.

All three fundamentals—standards, expectations, and goals—exist in other people *and* you. All three can be bent, changed, and even lived without, but you probably won't be very happy if there are remarkable adjustments to what you truly desire. See the list below for how a standard can set up an expectation or become a goal. Notice that the time period or outcome may vary, depending on where or how you started. Then write your own list.

STANDARDS | EXPECTATIONS | GOALS

As you move through the list below, notice all three attributes usually link together by the path they follow. Although, the fundamentals are separate. In other words, your standards are your starting point. Then, watch them grow into what you *expect*; positive, neutral, or negative. And finally set a goal for what you want to see happen.

Setting standards helps you set goals that coincide with your needs. Completing your chart will take some time, but if you make the effort, your visual aid will guide you throughout life. Whereby, proving to be worthy of your time in the long run.

Look over your list after a date or during a moment of clarity. Track any differences in your ongoing situation or relationships. Take notice to where you were *then* to where you are *now*. Perhaps there was something missing or a wonderful moment that happened in your interaction. Your date had a kindness about him, your career went in a new direction, or you decided you weren't expecting enough out of life. Update your list!

Another way to make your list useful is as a mediator while talking to your mate about the future. Keeping the conversation more regimented allows both of you to know if your needs will be met in the process. Being more of a form that needs to be filled out makes the uncomfortable subjects easier to talk about, too. As you go through this process, share what you need to. Then, be patient. Not all of what he wants will be to your liking, and vice versa, so prepare yourself to make compromises. See what you can and cannot live with.

For those single and dating: Talk over your list with your mate and see if you're compatible, *before* making a huge leap into a set future. How can either of you know if you should make a long-term commitment if you don't know what the other one requires? If you're not too far along into dating him, use your list to sum up if he meets your criteria.

For those in a relationship: Use the information that your list provides to discuss any changes you'd like to see happen. Maybe you need more out of the relationship, or you feel your life needs an update.

Assess your life and the people currently in it. Who and what do you want in your plan? What adjustments can your partner or you make to enhance your life? Review the examples below, and then create your own list. The list will become your guide for all future endeavors.

Also, pay close attention to how you word your items. Some standards may already be in place (e.g. you have a job versus you will get a job) so word the item in present tense when appropriate. Begin to live life with intention and discover how to love *with purpose*.

STANDARDS | EXPECTATIONS | GOALS
LIST OF EXAMPLES

STANDARDS - Your minimum requirements
EXPECTATIONS - What you anticipate getting
GOALS - Your future dreams and desires

Life Partner

S-He wants a committed relationship
E-He is committed to only me and wants to get married someday
G-I'll be married to a mate who has the same standards, morals, and values as I do

S-He is single or divorced
E-He is single, divorced, and isn't involved with anyone else
G-He has never been married, is committed to only me, and wants marriage with me

S-He has no kids
E-He has no more than one or two kids from a previous relationship
G-He will start fresh with me and build a family from scratch

S-He has a car
E-He has a good car
G-He has a classy car

S-He is family and friend oriented
E-He has a good relationship with some of his family members and he has a few good friends
G-Both of us are very family oriented, have great family and friends, and we want the same stuff out of life

S-He wants children
E-He wants at least one child
G-He wants to have ___ kids

S-He has a decent job
E-He has a good, dependable job
G-He has a great job making $___ a year

S-He lives on his own
E-He lives in a nice condo, house, or apartment
G-He owns a home in ___ (area) and wants to live ___ (area) when he gets married

S-He has religious beliefs
E-He shares the same or similar religious beliefs as I do
G-He shares my religion and has the same spiritual background as me

S-He has gentlemanly qualities
E-He opens doors for me, handles heavy tasks, checks my tires, picks me up for dates, and much, much more (list goes on depending on what details are important to me)
G-He always treats me like a lady and shows me respect. I feel loved and adored at all times

S-He cares about my well-being
E-He shows concern for my safety and well-being
G-He is protective, shields and defends me, but never tries to control me

S-He is average looking
E-He is good looking
G-He is great looking inside and out

S-He is respectful, loving, kind, and never abusive
E-He is respectful, loving, kind, and never abusive
G-He is respectful, loving, kind, and never abusive. He has never been involved in an abusive relationship, and I'm treated like a princess

S-He doesn't smoke
E-He only smokes at work; never around me
G-He is a non-smoker

S-We have a healthy sexual relationship
E-We have a satisfying, healthy sexual relationship
G-We have a quality, satisfying, healthy, incredible sexual relationship

Relationship (Personal goal)

S-I will date nice guys
E-I will date nice guys and probably a few bad ones
G-I will only date nice guys who are respectful toward me

S-I will be married
E-I will be married before I'm ___-years-old
G-I will be married before I'm thirty and will be married forever to my soul mate

S-I will have children
E-I will have at least one child
G-I will have ___ kids

Friendships

S-My friends and I are always respectful toward each other
E-My friends and I are always respectful toward each other, even when we have disagreements
G-My friends and I have respectful, kind, agreeable friendships and we're friends for life

S-I have a few good friends
E-I meet a lot of good people, have a lot of good friends, and have a few great friends
G-I meet tons of good people, have loads of great friends, and have special friendships that last a lifetime

Schooling

S-I have my high school diploma
E-I have my high school diploma, go to college, and will earn a degree
G-I have my high school diploma, go to ___ College, and will receive the highest possible degree in my field

Career

S-I have a job
E-I have a good job that I enjoy
G-I will have a wonderful career that I love. I will get all of the promotional opportunities that I desire.

S-I earn a good living
E-I continually increase my earnings as raises and promotions come about
G-I continually grow my education and earnings in a career of my choosing

Health

S-I maintain my weight
E-I am a size 8
G-I will be a size 6

S-I eat somewhat healthy
E-I will eat healthier foods
G-I will be a vegetarian

S-I smoke socially
E-I will stop smoking
G-I don't smoke

Material Possessions

S-I have a dependable car
E-I will have a good, dependable car
G-I will have a Porsche, Jaguar, or other car I love

S-I live on my own
E-I live in a nice place
G-I will own an elegant home in ___ (area)

S-I will have nice things that I love
E-I will be able to afford some nice things in life
G-I will have all the best items and live well

Now it's your turn. Grab a pen or pencil and start imagining all the details and guidelines you want from your life. Remember, the list will become your guide for all of your coming endeavors. Some may exist today, while others are what you want for the future.

    Don't forget to use the proper tense as you go through the list. Whether the standard exists in part today or begins in the future, either way, you need to have a higher goal set than what you have today. Take your time with the list and continue to add to it as you move forward. You will want to make copies of the list, before you get started, so you can add or change the items as you go.

STANDARDS | EXPECTATIONS | GOALS
YOUR LIST

STANDARDS - Your minimum requirements
EXPECTATIONS - What you anticipate getting
GOALS - Your future dreams and desires

Life Partner

S -
E -
G -

Relationship (Personal goal)

S -
E -
G -

Friendships

S -
E -
G -

Schooling

S -
E -
G -

Career

S -
E -
G -

Health

S -
E -
G -

Material Possessions

S -
E -
G -

The Mindful, Intentional YOU

Even if what you are doing today works for you, it's essential to stay open to what other opportunities life might bring to the surface. Every positive adjustment you make in your plan brings a new plan; one with possibilities of a bigger and better outcome.

Now is the time to take stock in what is important to you. Your list is your map to more success. Creating your list of requirements and desires pushes you in that direction. As you grow and evolve, your list will take on new shape and adjustments.

Keep in mind, happiness isn't always dictated by where you go in life, but who you have beside you, cheering you on in everything you do. Most importantly, hold onto your faith that everything will work out as it should, and stay open to the possibilities that present themselves.

IF I ALWAYS DO AS I'VE ALWAYS DONE...

As with many coined phrases, "If I always do as I've always done, I'll always get what I always got," we see the common sense of it all, and still we don't always follow the right path. We may find ourselves complaining about our situation, or lying dormant while life passes us by. Whether it is a relationship, a career change, or those other choices we make in life, we all land somewhere. It's our choice how we handle it.

I have pondered that phrase for years. The words give me great encouragement when on the rocky road to somewhere. Change can be perplexing, that's for sure. The challenges we face make us stronger; this we all know. As anticipation builds, the adrenaline in our bloodstream gets our thoughts flowing.

To create change in the *right* direction, we first need to get a little organized. If the idea of making a goal list sounds familiar, it's because it works! Having the ability to see, on paper, what makes you tick (happily) is to do what they do in business. Make a business plan!

If you took the time to make a list it does two things. Just as in business, it creates a goal; a place to go. How many businesses still do this today? It must work! That is, of course, if it's a *good* business plan. Then, as the juices start flowing in your brain, your thoughts begin to pour out into the universe. Now you have the universal energy working in your favor...and everything is *as it's meant to be*. Both of which, having a list and having conscious thoughts, are crucial for obtaining success in life.

Create one list or break it down by a variety of topics. Until you make copies of the SEG (*Standards, Expectations, and Goals*), start now with a simple piece of paper; writing down what comes to mind. If you're already making plans to get somewhere, that's great! Now, add a few more to your list.

Years ago, someone told me to make a list of what I wanted out of a relationship. I needed to know the characteristics I desired; personality, loyalty, trust, appearance, and peace. Notice I said peace.

Not something I would think to write down then, but would moan the word under my breath during times where patience was needed. Now, I see how critical peace is to my happiness.

A few years back I found my old list. I was thrilled to know that I had received much of what I wrote back then. It was a tiny piece of paper; so small you could carry it in your wallet. Since I found said note, I have misplaced it…again! Ugh! How is it that someone who is trying to tell you that a list is so important, then says she misplaced her own! That's true, but imagine how much more I could have accomplished if I held onto that small piece of knowledge.

One thing for certain is that *my goal* is to inspire people. I want them to reach out and enrich their own realities, and build up their self-confidence. I want them to take the best of themselves out into the world. My hope is that people begin to uplift their own self-esteem; taking steps to enhance their lives this very instant! I want to see palpable changes in the way people treat each other…and themselves.

When you share with others, or ask a question of yourself, you become a greater source of knowledge. That can change the way of the world…one person at a time.

"If you always do what you've always done, you always get what you've always gotten." That was the advice of Jessie Potter, the featured speaker at Friday's opening of the seventh annual Woman to Woman conference.

LOVE AND LIFE: TIME FOR A CHANGE

Many of us believe that certain seasons, such as spring time, bring the idea of hope and new beginnings to our lives. Then, there is the other side of that notion. What if those periods bring shadow, doubt, and confusion to your situation? What if you become bored or second guess your life choices? You think you need something new in order to be happy. That's very easy to consider when you think about it. Take a moment and think about how you feel during times of new seasons.

If change scares you, or you put the wrong emphasis on what truly needs to change, *those* emotions could be inaccurately shaped by your past or present. It all depends on how you look at change…the one happening in the moment. Maybe *you* need a change. And, maybe that change is *in* you.

Are you looking around you to see what, or who, needs to change? Does your life feel like it's not working anymore? Maybe, just maybe, you need to look in the mirror, instead of around you. Maybe the adjustment begins with you. I only ask you to think about it. I know I do at times.

It's easy to see what's missing in someone else. Most of us are pretty good at pointing out each other's faults, aren't we? And it's with great certainty that you will need to alter your circumstances at times, but first, look at the whole picture.

What's scary to conceive is this fact. What if that link, that unhappy, unfulfilled feeling sits inside you? It truly is something missing in you! There is a piece that no one else can fill but you. Sounds like work, doesn't it?

If you are missing passion, smiling, or laughter in your life, maybe the lack is within you! Could you *own* the fire that isn't creating a spark? Just consider it. Everyone needs to at one time or another. Maybe *you* are the one holding onto the past. Perhaps, *you* are looking for something, or someone, to fulfill you and make you happy?

Sorry to say, but you have to do that for yourself. Situations are what you make of them. You own the right, and responsibility, to do your best wherever you stand. Change and adjust as you need to.

The right change comes when you work on you. And since you can't change anyone else, that's perfect! As you continue to make healthy adjustments, you will learn what needs to happen. You can start to approach life in a more positive way. You will instinctively know your efforts are worthwhile. You will be happier…and the encouraging reaction from others won't hurt either. Your life will finally be changing.

Here's the deal. Do your part to put your best foot forward, and leave others to figure out their own spark. Hopefully, with a little effort you create a fire in you *and* them! Just know that you will be doing a huge favor to everyone by working on you in every situation. If you focus on you, and leave the rest to what other people own, you end up on the happier side. If not in the moment, then right down the road.

You will see that being happy isn't as hard as you once thought. Who knows, you might be the ignition that another person needs! It's very possible, you know. Have the best of spirit showing; now and in the future. Do your best to enjoy whatever it is that's right in front of you.

YOUR INTENDED GOALS

As mentioned a few times now, having a goal list is a necessity. If you haven't thought so, I beg you to please reconsider. A goal list is actually your intention list. When you put your intentions out there, chances are what you envision becomes your reality.

Consider creating a vision board and focus on it regularly. As you begin to visualize what you want in your lifetime, your attention gives you more power to attain them. Surround yourself with the message; on the wall, in your wallet, and on your desk. This is called the Law of Attraction and it is powerful.

Wait for what you want with anticipation and thrill. Yes, of course, always live in the moment and continue living your life as you should. Still, it's wonderful to get excited about the prospects of what is coming your way. You don't have to know all of the details of how or when something will occur. You simply hold onto the idea that *it* is coming.

- Want a better relationship? Speak it…act it…BE it.
- Want to have a great date? Expect it, know it, and show it.
- Want a new, even better job? Pray for it, look for it, and yearn for it.
- Whatever it is you want, *expect* you will have it.
- The sky's the limit.

As you already knew before reading this, not everything you want or *expect* will come to fruition. But you most certainly have a better chance of getting what you want when *that* is your intention.

Be more aware of what's going on around you. Enough that you search for the meaning of what is happening…in the moment. Those simple instances, like the unexpected phone call or meeting, or the delay in traffic that makes you miss your appointment time. Or maybe it's the relationship that didn't work out, or the guy or gal who simply got away. Everything is being done for your own good.

I know, sometimes it doesn't feel that way. You have to trust what you are putting out there, and more importantly, what God wants for you, is happening in the exact order it is meant. When you keep a positive outlook, God will continue to work wonder in your life.

I see it, experience it, and live with His intentions every day. Since I am only human, I stumble, and even fall at times. It took me a while to *get it*, but I know it to be true. You have to put your best self out there to get the best back. Pay mind to what is on your mind.

So stand up against the idea that you shouldn't have any expectations. Have those expectations for you and your life; today and in the future! It's really okay!

CHOOSING CONSCIOUSNESS

Unconscious choices are when you do or react in any given situation without thought. On the other hand, conscious choices are where you think about a situation, look at your options, and then make a decision. Right or wrong, good or bad, you are making the *conscious choice* to speak, do, not do, or behave in a certain way. You are heading toward that chosen choice.

There are times when being unconscious is relatively okay, but with some consequence. Like those times when you are washing your hands. Since you know how to wash your hands, you don't even have to think about it. Consider all of the tasks you do without even thinking. And that's fine; wash away!

What you miss out on is clarity of the event. You miss out on the appreciation of everything that goes into washing your hands. You have the water flowing through your fingers, the soap making your hands feel slippery and soft, and you even miss out on the action of putting your hands together in sync. Can you live without all of that action and still go on? Of course, you can! I only want you to think about these simple moments. Washing your hands is a small example, of course, but now I want you to think much bigger!

Look at a time when a child is talking to you. Are you paying attention to their words, looking into their eyes, and taking care to appreciate how they are feeling? Perhaps you're having a conversation with a friend and you're listening, but not really looking at them. Maybe you could actually *see* and *feel* their joy, their excitement, and maybe even their pain simply by looking deeper into their eyes.

Try it out the next time you talk with someone…or while you're washing your hands!

5
Cause & Effect

"How people treat you is their karma; how you react is yours."
~ Wayne Dyer

AFTERTHOUGHT

Karma can be a bitch, but, then again, she can be totally awesome, too! I have learned that what I put out there, I get back. So, if I want blessings to come my way, I better give my best self to the world. I need to set my mind to be a loving, caring, considerate, appreciative type of gal.

Don't be fooled! My attitude doesn't always behave. I can get irritable when life brings me new unexpected challenges. I am human. I make mistakes. Still, I am aware. The key is to continually work to get back to a place of being more grateful. I can actually feel the difference when I get wise to what I need to do.

On another topic, I discovered that I don't have to argue every single point. I mean, when it comes to politics, religion, money, and especially, other people's choices, I don't have to engage in the conversation when the situation isn't to my liking. I can keep my opinion to myself!

When I do decide to share my thoughts, I understand that just because someone doesn't agree with me, I don't have to change how I feel about the topic. They don't have to either. If they won't take my well-intended advice, that's totally up to them. Whatever the topic, if it doesn't make a difference in the grand scheme of things, I can *choose* to see and interact to it differently.

NEWTON'S THIRD LAW OF MOTION:
For every action, there is an equal and opposite reaction.

Newton's Law, Karma, Cause-and-Effect, God's Law; all are different, but very similar. They all come with their own set of rules, but ultimately they have the likeness on how you react to life.

When you think about energy, think about you. Every action, thought, and feeling goes into making the energy that embraces you. Others create energy around you, too, but yours is the only one you control. With that said, you can change the energy around you simply by putting your best inner self out into the universe.

Flash back to a time where you changed the conversation, altered someone's mood, or transformed your day. You *changed* the energy you generated at the time! There are easy and effective ways to test this theory of energy transformation.

Head down the street; waving at every person you pass. Send someone you haven't spoken to in a while an *I love you* text. This will surely make their day. As silly as it might seem, even complimenting someone on their tie or dress during a conflicting conversation can bring bad energy down a few knots.

The easiest way to expand your energy into a more positive manner is to hesitate. Pause. Think before you take action. Stop and clarify your intentions. Also, walk with the confidence that your purpose is for the good.

When you react well to situations, you improve the energy you put into every given situation to one of good, moral, and decent. You can be sure goodness will return to you in some way! Intention is everything. God works *when* you leave it to Him. And not until!

THE UNIVERSAL LAW OF CAUSE AND EFFECT:
EAST – Karma | WEST – The Golden Rule

I find the words we use in life interesting. We grow up believing one thing, and as we get older, we learn something new about those longstanding words. That, in turn, changes how we see all the other little words and sayings that are running around. I especially enjoy words from other areas of the world. Particularly, the ones I'm not familiar with. And even though the word doesn't match mine, they generally have a similar meaning.

For instance, Karma and the Golden Rule: two very different words but with similar meanings. In the west, we live with teachings of the Golden Rule, "Do unto others as you would have them do unto you." In the east, your actions, words, and thoughts will return to you in some way.

Growing up, I felt the rule was my big reminder that I needed to treat people how I *expected* them to treat me, or it will come back to bite me. Never once did I give thought of the other person and their Golden Rule! For some reason, I guess it only applied to me. Maybe I was so far removed from understanding intention, and cause and effect, that I just didn't see it.

Since then, I have discovered an even broader way of looking at the labels we use without question. I still believe whatever I put out there, I get back…but that's not all! Whatever I am getting, chances are it's because of what I (and maybe my ancestors) have put out there in my past. Yikes!

What I can tell you is that when someone or something wreaks havoc in my life, I stop and ponder for a moment. Could this be my past catching up with me, so to speak? I don't fret. I don't judge. I sit with it for a minute. I hold onto the lesson that *everything happens for a reason* and then, I move on.

> "You don't get everything you want. There's a price for whatever you get. And sometimes other people have to pay for it."
>
> ~ K Mitchell

Clearly, I don't believe everything bad that happens is my fault. That would be silly! I mean, look around! Maybe it's someone else's karma that I am part of in some way. I could be experiencing the karma of my spouse, parents, or a dear friend of mine. Anyone! Energy is everywhere.

I watched a program where Gary Zukav talked about karma. The idea was 'whatever you do unto others is *already* done unto you, and *that* is karma! You can't get away from it and you can't escape it.

There's another part of this belief system, too. It's that you must treat other people the way you would like them to treat you… because they will. You need to give to the universe what you want to receive back…because you will. The most fascinating part is that what you get back may not necessarily be from the same person or in the same way.

Years can go by before you ever reap what you sow. *That* is the beauty of its lifelong value! This is why living a good, kind, generous, helpful, moral, service-minded life is important. What you give, you get!

While the goodness you've given to others is great, the other side of karma is also thriving. You get the negative of what you gave, too. If you betrayed someone who put their trust in you, later in life, you could find yourself being deceived in another way…by someone else. And it hurts just as much.

Once you recognize the power of cause and effect, you will comprehend your experiences in a different way! You see, therefore, you don't take it so personally when someone betrays you. It was bound to happen. You know that you get what you give.

As I listened intently to Gary Zukav talk about this very subject, I tried to capture some other aspects of what he said. Here's part of it:

"The first thing you can understand is that there is a factor of karma involved. The other thing you can understand is that the person, who is acting in that way, is acting from a frightened part of his personality. He or she is in pain.

You never really have to worry about someone who does harm to you or creates an atmosphere of betrayal, because the karmic debt that they will have to pay; it will take care of itself. You don't have to take on the role of judge and jury.

What other way could you learn to create changes in you so permanent, so deep, so constructive as through your own experience in countering the consequences of your own choices? Until finally you stop trying to use other people, you stop trying to blame other people, you stop shaking your fist and blaming the universe. You stop curling up into a ball and wanting to die. You stop trying to impress everyone. You stop everything… and when you do, you create authentic power.

And when you keep following that path, it will eventually, as the saying goes, "bring you to your knees." Then, you are open for the first time because everything else you've tried hasn't worked, and you know it's not going to. The pain killers, the drugs, the wealth…it doesn't matter. That point comes when you open yourself, and when you do, then, change is possible."

I must admit, I remember specifically the first time I was brought to my knees. God had become a big part of my existence (finally) and I knew I had allowed evil to enter my space. I made a bad choice. I asked God to forgive me for my sin, and I've never forgotten the impact of that day. I don't know if I've paid for all of the bad karma I've put out there, but I certainly hope so.

Today, I live with the *intent* to never do anyone wrong. I don't go out of my way to hurt anyone; not even strangers. Still, I know that although some of my betrayals were a secret no one else knew, I believe, with every fiber of my being, that God has always been watching.

So go out into that big world and prove yourself to be worthy of good karma. Live by the Golden Rule, and let peace surround you.

Gary Zukav: www.seatofthesoul.com

POLITICS, POLITICIANS, AND WORLD EVENTS

Strange title in an intention book, I know, but here it is! I have a point for adding this section, so please read along with me.

I still remember the first time I was going to vote. As a young, inexperienced woman, that made for a very trying decision. As with many young adults, I was busy tending to my own life and what mattered most to me. I knew very little about politics or politicians. I was naive to what government did for our country and what the outcome could mean.

In the meantime, since politics was completely foreign to me, I decided to ask my parents if we were Democrats or Republicans. I was a daughter who fully respected her parents' opinions, and decided that whatever political side they were on, I was on. And that was how I voted.

As I got a little older, and a lot more independent, I educated myself more on politics. I soon realized it was okay to cast my vote anyway I chose. I could even vote Independent. Still, at the time I just didn't know any better.

Young people today understand fully that they have a voice. They can respectfully make their own choices in politics and in other touchy subject matters. People, in general, have chosen to respectfully agree or disagree when they have different opinions. Unfortunately, that's not exactly true. Some people forgot how to be respectful and kind. There have been big consequences for letting your position be known. To me, that is very sad. Those who don't allow sharing are not open-minded. They are not open to the idea that there could be another side. That can make the topic even more sensitive than it needs to be.

When you decide to discuss politics and world events, you could be opening up a can of worms. It all depends on who you are talking to. If two people have really strong beliefs or parties, the debate can get quite heated. Sometimes that heat can be a good, healthy discussion, while other times you should refrain completely from getting that conversation going. Stirring up the topic is simply too controversial for some of the parties involved.

I have been part of conversations that were very informative and refreshing, and I also have been part of discussions that have gone too far. Now, I only partake in debates as long as both opinions are respected. If either party is getting flustered over the discussion, because we believe differently, I stop sharing further points of view.

It's not that I don't enjoy going back and forth on a topic. However, if I'm dealing with someone who is closed-minded to any thought-provoking conversation, I don't feel it's necessary to argue the point with them any further. They can believe what they want and I can do the same.

As times get tougher for people, tempers can flare and emotions can rise. Election times can bring about a real desire for change. We rely on our government to protect us from harm, and then we get frustrated when the protection doesn't happen. I think, as time moves on, we'll see that we must begin with ourselves.

That said, most of us believe government needs fixing, but many do nothing about the issues except complain. You, as most people do, probably feel some discontentment, and even anger, with all of the drama. The way the economy, human interest issues, and global concerns are handled can be very challenging and disheartening. Not to mention, corruption is long-winded in government. I, for one, don't support adding anymore of that to it.

For those who do voice their opinions in order to see change occur, more power to them. Those *change-makers* get actively drawn in to create transformation in the way government and business runs our country. I see people actively involved in conversation, marches, and other events that involve the major issues. They want to find the solutions essential to gain more peace around the globe. If it's done respectfully, and for the greater good, I wish them much success.

While talking about *change-makers*, how many times have you heard someone say something needs to change, but it's going to take someone with influence for the issue to get resolved? I've heard it a lot over the years. Actually, if you watch television, read a newspaper, or surf the internet, you do see more people, including children, making big differences in the world; simply by getting involved. Every one of us can make a difference.

I do have one question to anyone trying to create change. Do you think it would serve us best by taking time to reflect on change *before* we make it?

Change is a process. You either make changes consciously or without much thought. You probably could list some of the hasty personal decisions you've made. Those bad choices you've had to live with for years. If only you had taken a little time before incorporating some of those personal changes. Would the outcome be any different today?

Stop and take the time necessary to see what you have to offer to the greater cause. Your deed may be as easy as dropping off items to a family in need, volunteering your time to support a cause, conserving energy, or comforting a person in need. Take a moment to see how you fit into the world's needs. If you begin to make some of the necessary changes, you will see that you actually have more power than once thought!

So, my reasons for sharing this section are two-fold. First, I wanted to get you thinking about those conversations that generally head to a bad place. Next, I wanted you to think about what changes *you* could make to conquer the problems of the world. In some way, you have to be accountable to yourself. More importantly, you need to be accountable to God.

Know that times will constantly change. Different leaders will carry the torch. That being said, if you want to see necessary changes, you will need to actively participate…respectfully. And remember, although politics, money, religion may stir up passionate debate, that doesn't mean it should interfere with your relationships.

WHAT SUPPORT LOOKS LIKE

Support comes from many different places, in many different forms, and from all sorts of people. The help you receive can be physical, moral, emotional, or financial in matter. It can come from family, friends, and even strangers. And, for now, you may not know if you'll need one or all of these support forms during your lifetime.

Let's say you need financial help from a parent or friend when tough times occur. Maybe you expect child support from a relationship that didn't work out. Perhaps, you are a parent looking for a little backing with the rules or needs of your family. Then again, the assistance you need might be for a little moral or emotional support from your mate or a close friend. There will be times when your circumstances or endeavors create the need for some support. Whatever help you need, there are rules to abide by when requesting someone's help.

With the exception of a few instances, all forms of support need your intentional thought? For one, you have to determine if you are showing respect to the person you need at the time. How are you treating them? How much, and how often, are you requiring their thoughtfulness? Second, consider if you are giving back to them in some way. The day will come when the kindness shown to you must be repaid in some way. Your return may be in the form of money, performing a task, running an errand, or a mere kind gesture that shows how much you appreciate them.

Albeit, you don't want to have expectations when you give to others; always expecting something in return. However, you don't want to be taken advantage of either. You should give when you can, and when appropriate or possible, get something back. If the return is not from them, it may come from someone else. Support comes in many different forms; a caring gesture, a helping hand, money, objects, or just being a shoulder to cry on. You never know how you will receive payment. It can come in other ways and from other people, too.

6
Intentional Gratitude

"Find a trinket to hold during times of conflict. Remind yourself that God is in control and you have very little to say about it. All you can do is be the best you can be. In these times of reflection, sit back and account for who you have become and what you've accomplished...for God."
~ K Mitchell

AFTERTHOUGHT

If you don't appreciate what is given to you, chances are less will be received. That's just my take on it. When life isn't going my way, maybe it's because I'm not being grateful for all I have today. I may be unaware that my actions, thoughts, or words are hindering what God is sending my way.

The day I figured out how to look at moments differently, with more intent, was the day my life came into perspective for me. This doesn't mean I don't have bad days in the mix. Still, I can remind myself of my power and ability to get back to a place where I am more peaceful and grateful.

I see people differently. I can look at someone and see them as a four-year-old, or I can see them as they are in front of me. This varies depending on how conscious I am at the time. Do I want to put in the effort to see them for who they really are; flaws, hurts, heart, and all? Or do I merely want to have a simple conversation? It's up to me.

I see other things differently, too. I can pick up a rock and see the beauty of it for its shape, color, and size, or I can just see a rock. It depends how intentional I am being in the moment. With that said, all rocks are special to me these days because I search for heart- and cross-shaped rocks. These days, I paint them just for the fun of it! I make plain rocks into something more beautiful. Today, I have a gratitude rock garden that I created with my grandchildren. I started it as a way to teach them about being grateful. That may sound silly, but it's not. They will remember this garden forever.

Actually, the gratitude rock is a thing! I even watched a story on the 2006 film, The Secret, about a man who made a big difference with rocks. These days, I see social media groups started for the sole purpose of children finding and painting awesome rocks. How cool is that! Spreading the love! And teaching children gratitude is one of the best gifts you have to offer them.

Finding the better of what life has to offer is found by looking for it. You can find beauty in your everyday tasks, your job, and even in your most loathed responsibility! You simply have to look for it.

Know this: everything will not go your way, nor will everything stay *just peachy* all of the time. Yet, if you make an effort to bring yourself back to a place of feeling blessed, you will find even more gratitude…for more reasons than you expected.

APPRECIATE THE JOURNEY

A friend once told me, "If you don't ever expect anything, then you'll never be disappointed." At first, I thought that sounded very negative and sarcastic. Then I realized it depends on how you perceive the message. There is another way to take the statement…and it has nothing to do with the expectations on your list.

If you ever thought of a time when you were really excited about an event or occasion coming up, only to be disappointed, then you know what I'm talking about. The time wasn't everything you imagined. You find yourself disillusioned with the moment. That's when expectations get messed up and put in the wrong place!

You might be surprised how truly exciting some occurrences really are when you stop dreaming about the future and live in the moment. Of course, you should have a vision and goals put in place for yourself, but you can't live in the future, only in the present time.

Between this section, and the list you created in Standards, Expectations, and Goals, you might get a little confused. First, I tell you to create a list of expectations; then, I tell you to have none. Read on and pay close attention to the explanation of expectations to clear up any confusion.

The shorter version is to live with expectations that are healthy; ones that don't cloud your mind with tedious details and disappointments. Take this tip. Go out on a date with the expectation that he treats you well and that you'll have a good time. Let the details of the evening play out as they should. Appreciate the details, but don't have expectations of them. Put good thoughts toward the evening, but don't plan every element. Consider the idea that you can think and speak your hopes and dreams about a time…even a lifetime. That is, as long as you don't allow those expectations to crush the spirit of those upcoming moments.

Many people believe you have the ability to speak your future into existence, even making a vision board with actual pictures of what you want out of life. I am one of them. But, you cannot let that vision discourage and dictate the occurrence happening in front of you. Believe you can have what you want, even *expect* it, but release your thoughts to the universe and go live your life.

To live with the notion that *someday* you will have everything you ever wanted, robs you of the wondrous miracles going on around you...at this very moment. Again, this does not mean you shouldn't allow yourself to consider some aspects of an event.

For instance, if you're giving a speech tomorrow and you want to prepare yourself for a successful day, envision what that looks like. With that, be sure to avoid the problems that can come with visualization. It's when the event doesn't go *as planned* (as you envisioned), and you find yourself disappointed. You can't allow that disillusion to interfere with how the remainder of the time goes. Take the time as it comes and know *everything happens for a reason*.

Consider the wonderful revelation of having no expectations of a situation and receiving the joy in whatever comes your way in that very instant. In time, you will be able to pull up this idea as situations present themselves to you. You will stop yourself from ruining whatever it is; reminding yourself not to place expectations on the details. You'll become more and more aware of all the bits and pieces around you as you practice paying mind.

Start appreciating your journey by paying close attention to the smallest of details in your interactions. Notice how you're becoming more connected in your daily routines and within your relationships. Soon, you will start to realize how happy you are because you know *how* to focus on the positive of each moment. The effort comes from inside of you, and you feel the gratification deep down to your core.

Life can't be taking for granted. You have to remain conscious of the fact that you are blessed! Once you learn how to be incessantly grateful for the wonders in your world, you'll start to see change happen.

MIRACLES: IN THE EYE OF THE BEHOLDER

Imagine you are gazing at a rainbow that covers the sky. Starting at one end and reaching as far as you can see. Maybe you see a beautiful sunrise coming over the horizon. The view inspires you to see amazing grace span across the heavens. In that moment, you realize the universe is so much larger than yourself. The entitlement you may have felt now moves toward a humble devotion. Nature has just given you a wonderful opportunity to see what is actually real. You witness the enchanting display and understand that *it* is the true miracle and a moment to be cherished.

Being able to witness the arrival of a new life coming into the world is undoubtedly one of my favorite miracles. I've been fortunate enough to witness two precious babies being born; my grandson and niece. I've experienced the onset of a mother meeting her foal for the first time. The arrival of the Lord's greatest achievements is a marvel to observe. I feel honored that I was present for the occasions to see what He can do.

There are so many miraculous occurrences on this planet. Like seeing how doctors can make a baby's heart grow stronger simply by placing a balloon in his heart. Or that the sight of a child can be restored through the *eyes* of another. To be witness to such events is a true blessing.

Some people have only been blessed to see a few wonders in their lifetime. And with all of these extraordinary sensations to be in awe over, you might find yourself curious about the true meaning of your existence. Have you observed any miracles? Did you think about how massive our universe is? Or were opportunities there, but you didn't take the moment in at the time? Maybe you weren't attentive enough to recognize the ones being presented. Hopefully, since you're now more aware, you'll recognize the depth of the miracles being offered to you.

What you do with the wonders you've been blessed with *is* what matters. Most of the time, after experiencing one, people go right back into their routine. They're glad they captured the moment, only to find themselves thinking about whatever they were doing before that spectacular instance. They might speak of the miracle, but they don't learn the lesson. You have to look *deep* enough to experience a wake-up call to create real change. Once you do, you'll want to create the habit of seeing more with other entities, too. Like the child who is babbling words to you; only to keep your attention. Look deeply.

If you're fortunate enough to capture even some of the special times that show themselves, and keep them as a daily reminder, you will become even more blessed. You will create a condition where negativity isn't allowed to wreak havoc over your entire day.

Speaking of incredible times, have you ever had the feeling of being fearless and free? I remember feeling that way when I looked through a pair of Blu-blocker sunglasses. These were very popular back in my day. They made everything around you look brighter and more beautiful. Another time when I felt fearless was while riding a roller coaster. The anticipation of me plummeting down the hill, my hands reaching toward the sky, while my bottom came off the seat was exciting! Think about a time when you had the thrill of a new experience, where you felt you could do just about anything. Pause now to reflect on one of those times.

Spend more of your time paying attention to the simpler details in life. There are many examples of how to love life *with purpose*. Pay attention to nature. Take the time to look differently at the flowers and trees, the sky, and all of the little critters surrounding you. Listen for the sound of your footsteps, or the smell of the lavender soap while taking a shower. Focus. Make an effort to enjoy them for their intricacies. Also, while you are paying mind, don't label what you see; simply see it. Naming what you are noticing takes away from the connection.

If you stand still and pay notice to even the everyday jobs you do, you will hear volumes. Live in the moments. I can't say that enough and you can't hear those words enough. Staying attentive and conscious as life happens. It is the key to your success.

FUTURE APPRECIATION

I had one of those undesirable jobs in the past. I worked for a company that went through a tremendous amount of change in the time I was there. It went from small business to big business within the first decade. With the company changing, there were also vast adjustments in my job description. Unfortunately, that became too difficult for me to take.

I went from buying the first pencil and setting up and managing the office, to filing insurance claims and collections. I can tell you with great certainty, collections is not the job for me. I started with building a challenging and fulfilling career, to a disappointing struggle of unsatisfying work each day. Plus, I felt my morals and values were being compromised by dealing with someone who was hypocritical and insincere to her coworkers. My hopeful dreams of a better career, along with my self-esteem, kept slipping away more and more each day.

Fortunately, the moment came when my mom showed me an advertisement in a local coupon magazine for a fabulous job. The company was offering a part-time call in secretarial position. Please understand, this was a reputable, quality company. I would be crazy not to apply for the job!

After a year and a half of waiting for a response, while I continued to endure a job I hated, I got the call. Months later, I went for testing, interviews, and was offered the job. Yay for me!

At first, I accepted the job. Then, I got scared. I had a life to support. I had limited financial resources and wanted to make the right decision. Would I get enough hours and make enough money to pay the bills? After all, this job required me to take a substantial pay cut! How many jobs would I have to have in order to make enough money? Out of fear, I called the hiring manager back and told her I couldn't accept her offer. Was I nuts!?!

After thumping myself on the head for discarding an opportunity of a lifetime, and weighing my options back and forth for a few short weeks, I realized what I must do. With hope that the position was still available, I called back and pleaded for the job.

Thank goodness the job was still open. Although she was apprehensive about my indecisive mannerism, she hired me. This great job was the best profession I ever had to date. That is, until writing, of course. If only I had listened to my gut…my intuition. I could have saved myself weeks of worry and disappointment.

When I started my new position, the first thing I noticed was how friendly people were to me. If you ever had a bad morning, just try walking down the hall, sad, while everyone who passes you wishes you a "Good Morning!" or "Hello, how are you?" Their attitude made you have a better day! How eye-opening it was to see how improving my attitude had the potential of creating a great day.

My work placed me at several desks of other administrators out of the office for a time; pregnancy, vacation, sick time. Although I never got settled in one particular place, this position became the solid foundation I needed for future opportunities that would come my way. I learned all of the various techniques each administrator used. This knowledge allowed me to pick and choose how I would run an office of my own. If my job would have been to only one desk, I wouldn't have received this great foundation. What a great opportunity!

After six months of spending time going from desk to desk, a manager approached me about a full-time position. She was offering me a job! I would create websites and other technical tools for her department! Yay! Since I had never created a website, I knew I had a long learning curve ahead of me. "Of course, we will train you," said my new boss. Great! Another opportunity!

This new position was unique, creative, and challenging for me. I loved it! I had multiple managers, great coworkers, and learning opportunities like never before. Better yet, my salary continually increased, as did my talents! Now, I could quit my second job!

I worked with so many talented and friendly people, and I was extremely happy. Once I created the department website, new design opportunities for tools became available, and my career options kept growing from there.

Later, I found myself switching to a behind-the-scenes technical position, where I helped others create websites and offered solutions on technical and software issues that came up.

Later still, I went to human resources where I continued to create websites, but also got to produce and present training materials. This new position even gave me access to Toastmasters and the employee diversity skills program. Bam! More great opportunities!

The moral of the story is if I hadn't been in such a bad situation in my previous job, I might not have ever left. If I hadn't left, I would not have found myself in a better place. I didn't need to be resentful or feel hurt any longer. I could look at it differently. I could be thankful for my new career. Not to mention, my improved self-esteem, pride, and self-worth. All of which rose to meet the occasion. Bear in mind, this is the third time that my unexpected career change was actually a blessing in disguise.

Try to find new ways to see whatever isn't working for you. Maybe it's a problem you've already reflected upon, but it's still not working. Consider the idea that future appreciations may exist right around the corner, too. Stay aware of what is happening around you. The answer could already be there. In conclusion, be thankful for some of the challenges and changes you go through. You never know where you will end up.

GAINING WISDOM

Another way to appreciate newfound, unchartered territory is to receive the gift of experienced people. Don't discard the opportunity to acquire some of that wisdom for yourself!

Folks who have been around for a while know stuff. Personally and professionally, they can save you tons of time and effort…if you are willing to devote some time to listen. Not everyone you know or every place you go offers that same consideration of their time and effort. Take advantage of it. As you start to notice more, you'll be dismayed at how others have no desire to help you get ahead in life.

I have worked for both types of companies. There are those with helpful employees and those with none, the ones with onboarding programs and others where mistakes are your guide. My corporate position was awesome; people helping people had to be their motto. Still, not every coworker is forthcoming with the details you need to perform your job. Trust me, I know.

I have shared many friendships on either side, too. There are friends who will listen; even asking questions about whatever is going on with me. Then, there are those who don't care anything about what's going on in my life. When you pay attention, you'll notice. I can say with great certainty that not everyone is willing to be helpful or compassionate. Be thankful when you find it.

When you have interested parties come into your life, those who made mistakes and reaped success, grab the opportunity. They're the ones willing to help you by listening, teaching, sharing, and giving. Both sets of knowledge, mistakes and success, are helpful to you.

All in all, you don't want to discard wisdom that is right in front of you because of what you *think* you already know. There will always be a time where you don't know everything. You have to understand that there is another side; one with greater possibilities. A side that offers you more hope or a new path.

Whatever isn't working for you may just be a paused moment. Look for the wisdom in someone interested in helping you through the details of it all.

TAKING TIME TO LOVE WITH PURPOSE

As usual, when a holiday comes around, we decide to look around us. We aim to discover all of the reasons we have to be grateful. So what's wrong with that? Absolutely nothing! This is especially true when we realize what each holiday means; beyond the hustle and bustle. Way past the gifts, get-togethers, and decoration.

Besides family, friends, and a roof over your head, what would you say is the real reason to be grateful? Hopefully, you said the Almighty. When you know God, Jesus, the Holy Spirit, and the soul that lives within you, you have found the true meaning of life. What is even more awesome is that you have these blessings surround you each and every day!

So why do we tend to wait for an event to recognize how blessed we truly are? Why do we wait to say, "I love you" until a tragedy occurs? Why don't we stop and smell the flowers that God gave to us? All I know is that if you want more out of life, you have to look at it differently. In order for you to have more, you have to see more.

Only secondary to being blessed by God are the people who surround you. Those who show you what it means to love another. When you offer gratitude to those who make your time here more incredible, that is an act that makes God proud.

When you wake up every morning, determined to look for reasons why situations transpire, your life becomes more meaningful. To clearly see why an event is unfolding, why someone showed up or left, or why you're handed a challenge, makes everything more interesting, too. Perhaps it's to wake you up. Possibly it's to guide you away from a horrible tragedy. Then again, maybe to offer you a lesson or blessing that leads you to the path you're meant to take. What I do know is that many of the tragedies I've experienced have manifested into some sort of lesson.

Still, as much as I would like to change some of the sadness in my past, I know it's not possible. I know it shouldn't change. Losing my sister, mother, grandmother, or grandfather are certainly events I would like to adjust, but I know God had to take them when He did.

It was not according to my plan. Do I understand? No, I do not. Do I have faith that there was a reason? Yes, I do.

Here's what I do know with certainty: God has a plan for me and everyone else. He knows what He is doing. I live each day with the understanding that I'm not in control; although sometimes I try. When I catch myself trying to grab the wheel, I let go and hand it over to Him.

When my husband was being prepped for open heart surgery, I finally had to learn to let go. I recognized the newness in my thought process. Did I stop worrying? No, but I knew I wasn't in control of the situation. That gave me some peace. I knew he was in good hands. I should stay proactive, to make sure he gets the best care, but I didn't worry as much about every detail. I prayed, asked others to pray, and hoped that God would hear our request to keep him here…with us.

Through all of the twists and turns of this frightening event, I was being asked to handle some marketing opportunities for my book. Did I fret about it? No, I did not. Why? Well, it wasn't because I didn't care about the prospect of my writing. At first, I did try to handle the details. Then, quickly, I realized it was not right…not at this time. I knew I wasn't supposed to work on *my* goals. I was to be there…for my husband. Perhaps it was a test from God to see if I would practice what I've talked about for so many years. Maybe He wanted to see if I really meant what I said about loving *with purpose.*

Since I wasn't in control of what was going to occur, and since I cared about my husband more than opportunities, I didn't fret. I knew I was doing exactly what I was supposed to. I was certain any opportunity that was presumed to be mine would unfold in the time it was meant to. I was at peace with that part of my life.

Still, I was concerned about my husband, for me, and our kids. Deep down I believed everything would turn out the way it was supposed to. Not to mention, the way we wanted it to. I just didn't want to see him go through the pain.

When you decide to let go, offering yourself to God to do what He wants you to do, doors will open. You will have everything you need; regardless of whether you know it at the time or not.

The Mindful, Intentional YOU

When you pay mind to what is happening in front of you, you experience freedom. You don't stress over what you *think* you are supposed to be doing, and you actually learn to live more…in the moment.

Yes, you will need to prepare for certain meetings or work to complete the responsibilities you have, but recognize when God turns a corner *for you*. It can be life altering.

Do yourself a favor and pay close attention to the details of your plan. Start looking for why a situation changes, why your plans get altered, or when something occurs that is out of balance. Then, watch how you choose to react.

It's as easy as looking at stopped traffic in a different way. Maybe there's a reason why you are here and not ten miles ahead. Don't get frustrated when plans don't work out as you expected. It may be God putting you right where He wants you to be.

You can create change that makes you grateful every day…and in every moment. You simply have to look for the blessing, the lesson, or the reason. It's in there!

YOU LOVE LIFE | LIFE LOVES YOU

There are many times when I was conscious of miraculous instances. When I was younger, some of those times were spent on the back of a motorcycle. However, there was one particular ride I took with a date that I will never forget. We went through a spread of trees that were no different than any other I have seen. I can't tell you where we were because I got lost in the moment.

I lost sight…but gained new insight…on what surrounded me. What I remember is *letting go* for those few minutes. My surroundings were calm and exciting at the same time. I felt good inside. I was as free as a bird, and the world looked absolutely beautiful to me. The greens were greener and the blues were bluer. A peace came over me like no other. I was in harmony with the universe. Just as quickly, I remember coming back to reality with thoughts racing back into my head. Those thoughts we have every day that overcrowd our brains.

Since I was always a little apprehensive on the back of a bike *letting go*, especially on a bike, was very unfamiliar to me. I wanted to go back to that feeling of connecting with the world, but really wasn't sure how to make that happen.

Today, I can get back in touch with the feeling of being aware of the world by watching birds, or by devoting my mind to other simple pleasures. I can be driving, sitting alone and quiet, or working on a project. I can focus all of my energy toward gaining a more positive perspective. It doesn't happen all by itself. I have to look for it.

If I see a flock of birds flying, I say to myself, "There's a piece of God." This is a sentiment my grandson would echo to me when he saw birds overhead. The scene reminds me of *my* belief that we are all merely simple creatures made by God, and He is the true miracle in our lives.

You, too, might have one of these special occasions while driving down the road. Maybe you forget how you got from Point A to Point B because your mind was elsewhere. To determine if this feeling is a special one depends on where your mind is in *that* moment. If you are thinking about a past hurt, drudging up an old negative encounter, or going over what you need to tend to, then that is not a special moment. Rid yourself of this kind of experience...especially while driving! But if you are looking around at the beautiful view life has to offer, and you're drinking in the ambiance surrounding you, then you are probably in that wondrous space. Be careful! Don't forget your driving.

Go through time experiencing each instance with fascination. Look at the occurrence as if you have not seen it before; with no familiarity. A childlike awe for each endeavor will keep you focused on the moment in front of you.

Realize you only have about seventy-three-hundred days in the next twenty years. Don't waste a moment of it. Reposition yourself and stay as conscious as possible to all of the details happening around you.

GIVING THANKS IN A TROUBLED WORLD

You only have to turn on your radio or television to see how horrible circumstances have gotten for many people in this world. Between the government, big business, and troubled individuals, everyone is feeling the strain somewhere in life. For a lot of people, the amount of bad state of affairs is overwhelming to say the least.

As days go by, many folks wonder how they can muster up enough good will to spread around throughout the year. People are losing their jobs, homes, and families. In their dismay, how will *their* gratitude ever shine through?

The best you can do is put effort into helping in some way. Attempt to find that silver-lined cloud that has, if nothing else, hope attached to its future. Hope that tomorrow brings a brighter future. Hope that any present woes quickly come to pass.

In the words of the spiritual teacher and author of Broken Open, Elizabeth Lesser, you need to focus on three tasks per day:

- ♥ Find ten things to be grateful for every single day.
- ♥ Make it your business to learn something new about something or someone.
- ♥ Do something for someone less fortunate than you.

Just as with anything else you work to accomplish every day, you need to take the time necessary to work on yourself. Exercising, eating right, and creating a peaceful environment are only a few of the ventures that get pushed aside when life gets crazy. You know taking care of yourself is important, but you keep putting it off anyway. You need to create a new habit.

Imagine that you spent the afternoon creating a really good meal for yourself. Only to find you're stacking it on a paper plate as you run out the door to your next appointment. Now, you have to drive, eat your nicely prepared meal, and stay safe and clean…all at the same time! If you can't savor the great meal, what was the point in making it!

Make an effort to savor life as it comes at you. If you don't, before you know it, time has gone by. You won't get it back either. It's gone! Can you say with great certainty that it was time well spent?

While you aim for more quality time, find at least one minute a day to reflect quietly. Quiet your mind and find your center space within. Sit or lay with your arms to your side and your legs uncrossed. With an open frame, you are better equipped to take the good energy in with each deep breath.

Once a habit gets established, increase the time from one minute to five, then ten, and so on. You come out better equipped to handle the pressures of the day, and more capable to see how blessed you really are by the people and situations that surround you. You are able to filter the good from the bad.

Life gives you moments to do what you want to do. With all of the trouble in this world, spend some time finding the good in all you can. Do *your* best to bring good to people and situations by reaching for that silver-lined cloud.

Elizabeth Lesser, Spiritual teacher and author of Broken Open:
www.elizabethlesser.org/broken-open

7
The Give & Take of Relating in Relationships

"Through people, places, and situations, God is always reminding us that there is nothing more important than staying focused on the things that matter most. We must never forget that it is always the thoughts that we choose to entertain that become the distractions that drag us away to places where God never intended us to go."

~ Gary Woodson

AFTERTHOUGHT

This is definitely the longest chapter in the book. While I talk more about other people here, *you* are still the main focus. The goal is to look at how you react in your relationships. Plus, we have to talk about the negative side of life, too; those challenging moments that creep into your relationships. It has to be done!

The key is for you to stay mindful. Not everyone is here for your good. Not everyone will stand by your side in times of conflict or challenge. You have to listen to your gut. For me, I take the stance of *Guts & God* when trying to remain conscious to what is going on. Listen to my gut, knowing *that* is God, the universe, trying to pull me in the right direction.

It took me a long time to realize that if I would have listened to that little voice, the knot in my gut, I would have saved myself a lot of trouble. It's where intuition lives; my soul. It's the closest place I have to God, in my opinion. If I want to know what to do, I listen to my gut; hence, *Guts & God*.

Now, while you fend off any troublemaker coming to make your days less pleasurable, take a look at how you treat those who are here for your good. Think about those people who give you love and companionship. You've got your family, friends, and the other do-gooders in this world. Do you know someone you could show a little more appreciation to?

See how I turned that around! Yes, you must pay attention when it comes to people and situations as not everyone is here for your good. People will let you down. Still, showing up on the brighter side of thinking, finding what you should be grateful for, is a major plus. Just take new connections from wherever you are…in the moment. Go into circumstances with positive energy and let *Guts & God* handle it from there.

I know I can find myself busy and forgetful (unconscious) when it comes to *showing the love*. On a good day, there is always another chance to make it right. That's what I like about intention. There's usually another chance. If you put effort into making the opportunity arise, it's possible to change someone's day. And that someone might be you!

While you are staying all positive, don't think for a minute there isn't a cost to being intentional. Your life takes on a change. As *things* and *circumstances* become less important to you, you learn to discard much of what you held onto for so long. Your focus becomes much bigger, while staying mindful and holding onto your faith makes everything else seem so much smaller. You learn to look at *stuff* with a grain of salt. I really like that. Sure, there are belongings and people I put in my important box. Yet, I learned to abandon many of the trivial circumstances and items with much more ease.

Change is a growing process. It isn't just handed to you. Learning to stay mindful of the truth about everything makes for an interesting thought process. You end up seeing the matters of life in another way, whereby processing them differently. Almost as if you're standing there holding an "Important" sticker in your hand; waiting to determine the cost of each thing that comes your way. Cost takes mindful decisions. Make conscious choices that are for your good and not harm.

WATCH YOUR HEART

We should be thankful for all of the wonderful people who help the many lost souls. They are to be appreciated. With that said, notice there is *still* the other side of life. That side where people are inconsiderate for someone else's feelings, property, and situations. Not to mention, there is more violence and hatred than years past. Though some may not agree, to me, it is clear we have a lot of work to do to become a more positive, loving society. If the media is any indication to how people are doing, I think I'm right.

When I was a young teenager, it was safe for me to walk down a dark, desolate, neighborhood street. I didn't fear being attacked. Sure, there are still places offering that type of security, but I think the number is declining at a rapid rate. There is much more risk when deciding whether to go down *that* road when you're alone.

Maybe you know someone who speaks ill of other people behind their backs. Or they show disrespect to those who are talking by interrupting them. Perhaps someone you know, or you, has been a victim of crime. There are many cases of inconsideration and violence you could name. Clearly, you have to *watch your back* at times.

Between all of the business transactions you are involved in, and the personal relationships that evolve, you need to pay close attention. While interacting in relationships, be aware of two things: how you act *and* how others treat you.

For instance, you might make a large purchase where the merchant wants to make a hefty profit over giving you a fair deal. Maybe you have to compete for a promotion at work. In both cases, the other contender is counting on victory at your expense.

Whether you're engaging in personal or business relationships, or meeting new people, sometimes you have to determine *what's their purpose?* You have to understand the purpose of the engagement in order to understand the logic behind it. Maybe not with you, but someone somewhere is getting the shaft or making a deal for their personal advantage. Be smart, not pessimistic, when dealing with other people.

This all sounds quite negative, but it is realistic to assume you should be prepared that at some point in time someone will not have your best interest at heart. It's important for you to define if you should take an interaction personally, or waste any energy on figuring out why it's happening. Maybe the connection is supposed to go that way. Again, be smart, respectful, and remain positive in your exchange.

Having to interact with someone who doesn't have your best interest in mind may affect you in various ways. If the situation is a common business transaction, you may not be shocked by the other person's disloyalty to you. This is probably true when dealing with a vendor trying to earn a few extra dollars at your expense. That scenario probably wouldn't bother you too much. Now, imagine you are in a personal situation. For reading purposes, here is one of mine.

I remember my first *new car* purchase. My boyfriend was with me and I was having a hard time making a decision about whether to buy or not. After hours of negotiation with the salesperson, my boyfriend said, "Yeah, that sounds good," to whatever figure the salesperson gave me. That was easy for him to say, since I was the one paying for the car! I felt pressure from the dealer, I wasn't prepared to accept the offer, and now my boyfriend was siding with the seller! Who does that! I felt completely alone. Where was my support?

If you repeatedly experience the type of situation where someone deceives you, or doesn't support you, those connections change you. This can happen in business or personal matters. The circumstances can alter who you are in that instance…and sometimes longer. Once you identify the facts of your situation, you may alter who you negotiate your affairs with in the future.

Know who you are dealing with *and* who you are being…in the moment. Negativity has the ability to change you. The change may only be for a few minutes, affecting your mood during a business transaction. Or it could last a lifetime, depending on what you are putting up with and for how long.

Big or small, one of the leading concerns of negativity is what it does to your health and spirit.

THE RESULTS OF NEGATIVITY

Negative behavior also changes the person who is mistreating you. Somewhere along the way these negative souls have lost their way. They rarely check in to see how their actions affect other people. You may have a man at the age of thirty standing in front of you with a fourteen-year-old mentality on what is reality and true. Then again, you might be dealing with a friend who is fighting the stresses of life and she can't possibly worry about you. She doesn't even have all the answers for herself.

Another example might be a person who brings their work role, such as a warden or police officer, to a social setting where he continues to reprimand or police the person he's talking to. If not because of a work role, perhaps they are a victim of a victim. They are someone who is continually being disrespectful or dishonest toward others. They have been playing the tapes for so long, they are now on autopilot. They just do what they do. Then they justify their actions with excuses or defiance.

Moreover, negative circumstances change your culture. Each and every time you have to endure a negative situation you're affected in some way. When you go out into the world with that chip on your shoulder or with pain from past woes, you take all of that with you. If you're not aware of this baggage, and they step in your way, you have the ability to ruin another person's day.

Dealing with optimistic people and circumstances is always the best solution, but, of course, that's not always possible. When dealing with negativity, it's important to know these situations can mold your character. Either slightly by altering your spirit…in that moment, or radically, by changing how you operate or how you manage your standards. Most times, you have the capability to get past the unconstructive interaction and move on to the next point in time.

An example comes from years ago while I was at my father's condominium community pool. I met a guy! Almost immediately, I was attracted to this man. He was good looking, well built, and had the appearance of a man who had his act together. After a long conversation that day, we decided to go on a date. We had a good time and continued to see each other on a regular basis for a couple of months. He took me to nice places, had a good job, drove a nice car, and owned a condo. Or so I thought.

After dating a short while, I started noticing that he drank a lot. He would bring over a twelve-pack of beer and within a few short hours it was gone. After a couple nights of this behavior, I wondered if there could be other issues to consider. Now that he had my attention, I finally took more notice to his other traits.

He told me he traveled for work, so I knew there would be times when he would leave town for a few days. While he was gone, he'd call to check in, and we would go out when he returned. Aside from the couple nights of his excessive drinking, everything else seemed to be going nicely. Still, I had a feeling inside me that continued to question his sincerity.

On one particular evening, when he called me from a hotel, he happened to mention the town and hotel he was staying in. The next day, with the intention of wishing him a good morning, I looked up the hotel's phone number and made the call.

I was surprised to learn that he wasn't registered at that hotel, and there were only two other hotels in the area. Being suspicious of his behavior already, I called the hotels. Nope, no one by that name! When he called me later, I questioned him on his whereabouts. He swore he was there.

What was the outcome? Much to my surprise, he never called or came around again. He even moved out of his condo without so much as a word. Yes, about a week after our phone conversation, I went by his condo. All I saw was a pickup truck and a few people going in and out. I stopped to ask if they were moving his unit. The news came as quite a shock. He didn't own the condo, he was six months behind on rent, and he was gone without any notice! Wow, did I know how to pick them!

I realized then that he probably didn't work where he said, had a drinking problem, and who knows what else! I got over his deceit, but I did find myself angry for a period of time; because of all the corruption. Unfortunately, there are inexcusable exchanges that occur in life. Some of those interactions can change people to the core. This one did not. I had been through worse.

If you are genuinely an honest person, and you deal with someone who is always being untrustworthy, you will begin to change. You might adjust your individuality by becoming more suspicious, aggressive, spiteful, or angry. You could change how you are with that person, or you could become distrustful with other people you encounter. You do this as a way to protect yourself from harm. Still, it's not good for you or them.

If you continually deal with mean, uncooperative, untrustworthy, negative people, you undoubtedly will alter your view of people and the world around you. Usually, we have the ability to discern right from wrong and good from bad. We can tell when *we* don't follow good values. However, the same gets overlooked when figuring out someone else.

When you set aside your morals for your own gratification, that's when you get in trouble. When you continue on a path that doesn't fit well with your beliefs, you'll unquestionably change your reality. Your true identity will be concealed from everyone…even you. You will live in a way that defies your true beliefs and authentic character. You will become disingenuous.

On another note, some people have trust issues outside their small circle of relationships. I believe most people understand that issue. For others, the town or city they connect with regularly feels trustworthy, but reaching outside that comfort zone may cause them to suspect concern. While still others feel the world is their playground. It's all relative to the person.

Trust is a conscious decision you have to make. No matter what your thoughts are on trust, you should engage with strangers with an observing eye. Wait for your gut to tell you more, while staying fully aware of your position.

Being *observant* is a positive aspect of connecting with new people. Staying attentive helps you to look at the facts of a situation, without the judgment of first impressions. It allows you to consider if you should even interact with a particular individual or in this state of affairs.

On the lighter side of this conversation, you could get some satisfaction knowing there are people in your life who go to bat for you. They are the ones who fill your days with interesting and enjoyable moments. They got your back during times of need. They lend you an ear, give advice, or hold your hand. Plus, they appreciate and love you for all you are and what you have to give. And besides all of that, you trust them.

If you focus your attentions on the positive influences that surround you, you will see you are worthy of so much more than you knew. You just have to believe…and make conscious choices.

VALUING YOU

When you think about how you are treated by other people, are you disappointed, content, or satisfied with that treatment? Do you feel appreciated, respected, or loved? Depending on who you are talking about, the answer can range from fine to really horrible.

The trouble with being treated badly by anyone is that it could be contagious. When you don't *expect* respect and kindness from those you deal with, the problem just grows. First, you continue getting disrespected by them. Next, you start to believe that everything is okay. Then, other people start to disregard you, too. All of which is unacceptable.

In most cases, when it comes to how you are being treated, people will behave only in the way you *allow* them to. If you require someone to be respectful toward you, they either demonstrate that behavior, or they won't be permitted to interact with you. However, when disrespectful, ungrateful, or unloving dealings are allowed to continue, the situation undoubtedly will get worse. The problem can be with a particular person or in general. If you don't stand up for yourself, that low self-worth you feel will radiate from within and pollute your other connections.

Think about the people in you circle; those you *choose* to spend time with on a regular basis. Are they conscious, positive thinking people, or do they discourage you; spewing toxic negativity? Make note that attitude attracts attitude, and what you surround yourself with can be what you become. If you hear compliments or insults enough, you probably will start to believe it!

To elaborate, it is best to set yourself up in an environment that is positive and healthy. You will be a better person for it. Obviously, there are some people you have to stay involved with, like family, but that doesn't mean you have to soak in all of the drama. Nor does it mean you have to constantly accept what they are spewing.

For instance, if you have a teenager who is in constant complaint mode, you can tell them to take their chronic grumbling to the bedroom. This allows the rest of the family to remain peaceful.

Moreover, you don't have to sit and listen to the loud and disrespectful brother-in-law as he shouts about the government or speaks disrespectfully to his wife. You can avoid him, remove yourself from the room, or maybe take his wife with you as you go!

Certainly, you've heard the expression about how you must love yourself in order for anyone else to love you. There will always be people who love you unconditionally; your parents, children, or mate. Still, being the product of low self-worth will ultimately damage even those connections in one way or another.

You have to value yourself enough to *expect* respect. You have to love yourself enough to know when toxicity is taking over your thoughts and attitude…your life. If you don't value you, who will?

Be strong and courageous enough to look at what you are standing for. Then, take a stand where you need to. *Expect* to be handled with care from anyone who connects with you. Your mate, date, children, friends, and even acquaintances should treat you right. Demand respect, require appreciation and gratitude, and know that you deserve the best from all of your relationships…because you earned it. Know you are worthy.

JUDGING A BOOK BY ITS COVER

Stop and think about how you judge people based on appearance. We've all been judgmental at one time or another. Pay attention to those first few seconds when you encounter someone. You might be surprised to find that a person's appearance tells you very little about who they are.

Think about a time when you saw someone with a peculiar hairstyle, tattoos that cover their body, or clothes you wouldn't be caught dead in. How did you react to them at first glance? Stop and think about situations where you made assumptions.

What I do know is that I've met many biker dudes who are gentle giants, and I've met quite a few successful businessmen who are vicious takers, too. Anyone can make a presentable appearance, but that doesn't necessarily mean the person has good breeding.

To find out if someone is a good person you need to know their character. Only so much can be evaluated by first impressions. That is, unless someone is a real jerk right from the get-go. Some people aren't very good with first impressions. Being able to tell if someone is a good person may take some time when getting to know them.

When you meet someone new, consider if he or she meets your expectations of a good person. Continue on *if* there's an interest in getting to know them. If they don't turn out to be so good after all, then you can reassess your first impression.

Better yet, don't make a first impression! Then, there is nothing for that person to live up to. Take the burden off of them *and* you. Just enjoy the moment. In time, all you need to know will be revealed. In the meantime, this is one of God's children standing in front of you.

It all starts with taking care of yourself and those around you. If you handle interactions and situations with dignity and respect, most likely, you will have successful relationships. No one is perfect, you know, so make an effort to handle relationships with care. Give everyone the benefit of the doubt.

When you encounter obstacles, and you will, be self-sufficient enough to take care of your own needs. Address your own issues and ask your loved ones to do the same. Taking on responsibility for both sets of issues is not right. Actually, it's impossible. I've tried!

For instance, when I was growing up I was always insecure about one thing or another. I was insecure about my appearance (*am I thin enough, pretty enough?*). Plus, I wasn't sure whether I was accepted by my peers and siblings. I even talked with past classmates, who told me that they thought I was a snob back in school because I always had my head down. What's ironic is that I had my head down because I didn't feel I was *good enough* to hang out with them. They were *too cool* for me. Imagine how much more fun I could've had in school. If only I learned to feel good about myself sooner.

My issues began when my insecurities started lowering my self-esteem. I couldn't make my family, peers, or friends responsible for my confidence levels. These were my issues. My parents did the best they could. In fact, I'm pretty proud of them for getting through all of the drama three young girls can create. My other relationships couldn't fix my issues either. I showed up with this baggage. I needed to find my own self-worth.

Just as an alcoholic can't be fixed by an enabling codependent, an issue-holding woman can't be fixed by anyone else. Getting through issues takes time and a lot of work. No one can do it for you. You can get support in times of need, but most personal issues still need fixing from the inside.

When I was in my early twenties, a dear friend of mine, Joan, used to tell me "We own this place. Let's go have some fun!" She would say this right before we walked into a dance club or party.

I was introverted with very low self-esteem at this point in my life. I just got out of an abusive relationship, was feeling quite low about myself, and had never gone clubbing before. My friend was the exact opposite of me. She was very outgoing, bubbly, and ready to take in whatever life had to offer.

I didn't realize it at the time, but my friend was trying to get me to open up and feel good about myself. She was trying to break down my walls so I could lift my head high again. And her strategy worked pretty well! In time, I was able to use that simple phrase in other areas; when I was nervous or unsure. I began to see my self-worth rise and my true personality emerging.

At the time, I didn't know *how* to work on myself so my insecurities didn't rule me. This vulnerability still haunts me today, but generally only in times of major conflict. Otherwise, I feel pretty confident about who I am. My appearance and abilities are just fine. The idea of getting accepted into a group, or being liked by everyone, doesn't matter as much either; not as much as I used to think anyway. I know I will always be a work in progress, but I have definitely grown into the person I am proud to be. For one, I own the issue of my low self-esteem. I stopped trying to pawn my insecurities off on my parents and other people in my life. I made my own decisions and I had to live with those choices.

Eventually, even if someone else is to blame for an issue, you must own your part. If you had painful experiences as a child, and now you're an adult, then accept responsibility today for your actions. If you need help from a therapist, counselor, or person of faith, then go get the help you need. Take the stand that you'll look at whatever is going on. Do what needs to be done to make your future brighter.

So tell yourself, "I am worthy of my place in this world," and hold your head high while you speak it! Once you begin this ritual of self-awareness, you will begin to have a happier life.

WHAT YOU GIVE | WHAT YOU TAKE

Women, more than men, complain about being the giver in their relationships. You probably tend to pay more attention to every little detail, and person, before you think of you. You probably say or do what others want or need you to, simply because you don't want to cause problems or appear unkind. Today is the day you stop worrying about *always being nice* just so you don't upset the apple cart.

I'm not suggesting that you be hostile or unkind with your words or actions. Only that you make good choices and stand up for yourself; without feelings of guilt or resentment. Frankly, you shouldn't hold onto those feelings in the first place. You don't ever have to sign up for guilt. Once you stop falling for the refuge of guilt, others will stop trying to use it on you.

If you are one of those women who always give, while someone else always takes, stop and take a look at what you're doing. You have needs, too. Those needs should be met by your friends and family members. You should *expect* that as a standard. If you're in need, a loved one should be there for you. After all, you would show up for them if they were in need, wouldn't you? Now is the time to let others know you require the same in return. Express your heartfelt feelings in an open and honest approach. Let them know you have requirements. Tell them that you are happy to be there for them, but you need something in return.

You don't do anyone any favors when you neglect yourself. Before you know it, all of your strength and energy is zapped. Plus, people need to be needed. If you don't require that of them, then they are missing out on being a better person. They don't experience caring for someone they love. Moreover, they take this lesson to other relationships they encounter.

While there will always be people who need you, you have to require *mutual respect*. You do this by expecting and accepting the care and consideration of others in return. People do what works for them, until that behavior doesn't work anymore. A lot of times they don't even realize they are taking you for granted. Requiring more from your loved ones does everyone a favor.

Make a vow today to stop carrying the burdens of others. Begin to live for your personal fulfillment. You can have a respectful give-and-take relationship simply by creating that rule as a standard. Any meaningful change will begin with you. Reclaim your power and reposition your energy toward what you need.

Once you begin expecting more, the ball will begin to roll. You will create the change that eventually makes a difference not only in your life, but in that of your friends and relatives. You can even make a difference with those you call strangers. You're not being selfish. You're taking your fair share.

A GIVING PERSON RECEIVES

In chapter three, *Stand Out Above the Rest*, I talked about being your best self. You may be wondering what volunteering and giving has to do with your relationships. As I see it, this kind of behavior and actions enriches your life. It's also useful to seek these qualities in your family or a mate.

Someone who cares for other people, outside of his family and friends, is probably going to be more open to making a relationship work. He sees the bigger picture. He probably recognizes that putting in the time and effort to help someone else can help him achieve a better reality. The added bonus is he'll probably be more considerate of you, too!

Imagine being able to make *caring for others* a value in a child's mindset! These days even small children take on projects to improve the world. Some of the work these children have accomplished would probably overwhelm most of us.

For example, the little girl, Stephanie, who heard about an injured manatee through a newspaper article she read. She started making and selling manatee pins to raise awareness. Soon after, she turned her dream into a nonprofit corporation. *Kids Making a Difference*; an organization ran by kids, for kids. Today, this organization has grown to help even more animals in need.

Her drive and success should be motivating to adults everywhere. To know that even a small child with a big heart can make a genuine universal difference is powerful.

Kids Making a Difference: www.kmad.org

LISTENING MAKES ALL THE DIFFERENCE

Sometimes, taking time to really listen to someone else is hard work. The story might not interest to you, you're too busy, you have a point to make, or the person may go on and on. There are times when you have to make a mental note to yourself to wait before responding until the other person has had a chance to finish speaking their piece. Pausing for a few seconds, before you reply, tells the speaker you are actually thinking about what they just said. Nodding your head in recognition of their words can help justify that you hear them, too.

On the other hand, interrupting or responding too quickly tells them you weren't actually listening, or that you already had your mind set to speak or give an opinion. You can literally shut a conversation down if they think you're not listening, or when they get tired of trying to talk over you. Your rude behavior can make them feel unimportant and disrespected. Trust me; I've shut down many times when I don't feel heard. For me, it's just not worth the fight. I don't want to speak over people, nor do I want to waste my breath if someone isn't listening.

During those uncomfortable times of controversy, the ability to listen, instead of rushing to state your case, can make or break a relationship. When you don't think the other person is listening to your side of the story, you probably won't get past the conflict. Sure, you may find some resolution to the problem, but chances are the underlying issue remains until you feel you've been heard.

One of the best gifts anyone can give to another is to listen to them. Hear what they have to say. Show interest in what they are talking about. Be mindful to hesitate before responding to them. Ask questions to clarify a point, or elaborate on the conversation.

The gift you get in return is the opportunity to learn more about another person. Plus, you become less self-involved, and that's always good. You find you are more balanced because you took the time to actually learn what someone else thinks. Who knows! You might even learn something new that helps you!

PRIORITY CHECK

Be yourself, congratulate yourself, and trust your instincts. Seriously, just do you! While living your life, don't forget to tend to the details that are important to you. You have to make sure your priorities are in order. It's easy to get caught up in making everyone else happy, while dismissing your own needs and desires. Don't do that. Determine what you need. Then, go after it.

A mate who wants your love will be open to working out any details to improve your relationship. This includes making some compromises along the way…on both sides. A mate with the desire to make your relationship work, and the open-mindedness to compromise, will keep putting in effort until he gets it right. Your time will be filled with tears of joy, and tears of sorrow to some degree. Still, it's crucial for the two of you to take the time necessary to get the kinks worked out.

Finally, it is true that wealth doesn't buy you happiness and contentment. It's also true that money doesn't grow on trees. While currency does make life easier for you, it doesn't come close to the core of happiness. You have the ability to have so much more. You can have pleasure and contentment by building healthy and strong relationships. Connecting with your mate and other loved ones represents the largest part of your peace and happiness. To get to the point of continual harmony in your relationship requires effort from both parties. The outcome is worth your sincere efforts when you get it right.

FORGIVENESS 101

Look, we all make mistakes along the way. You can't beat yourself up for your mishaps anymore. If you did a forgivable act, your loved one will let your troubles pass. That is, once you make a sincere apology.

If you realize you have been handling your relationship poorly, make a vow to fix what you have done…or haven't done. No need fretting over the past because he *is* still with you.

If you believe the healing starts now, and you are on your way to making the changes you desire, then you will be okay. It is when you stand still, making no effort to fix what's wrong, that you will remain a little lost.

Think about what you have been through in your life. How much have you paid emotionally, physically, spiritually, or financially? Hopefully, you (or others) haven't paid too much on any one thing.

If there are matters from your past that you're not so proud of, apologize to yourself right now. Then, go apologize to those you have hurt along the way. Now, stop beating yourself up for whatever happened in the past! You cannot change it. If someone else did you wrong, learn to forgive them, and then *let go* of the matter.

Make a commitment to rewrite your history. Starting today, make the necessary adjustments to transform your life. Stop doing what doesn't work, and start *expecting* to blossom in your future. Stop living in your past. Be patient with yourself and enjoy the journey. While you cut yourself a break, make sure you aren't still making someone else pay for what has happened in your past. "*Ex malo bonum*," is Latin for "out of bad comes good." Hence, take care of those connections in need of repair.

If you look at your past mistakes or pains as learning experiences, then they're a lot easier to swallow. In fact, some elements that make life hard are blessings in disguise. Perhaps you have a better job today *because* you quit that undesirable position. Maybe you discovered new information that changed the facts about a situation. You holding onto the issue only took longer for the truth to be revealed. Whatever your blessings, whatever your lessons, forgive what is done.

GIVING A HELPING HAND TO A HAND IN NEED

Recently, a large order of my books came to me with printing issues on the cover. I was devastated because I knew I couldn't sell them, nor could they be given away without covers on them. For me, this was a real waste of good material.

Since I never throw anything away, I wanted to see what I could do to make these books presentable to someone who could use some good relationship advice. After all, the content was still there so why throw them away!

I knew my passion was to help young women in trouble, but I wasn't sure who. Who could I give these books to? Who would want them? So I waited and waited until I knew in my gut who to help. Who pulled at my heart strings? Not to mention, I still needed to figure out how I was going to fix the covers and at what cost!

Turns out, it was easy! Thanks to the help of someone I met through my journey of writing, Doug Heatherly, the owner of Lighthouse24, I was able to reprint the covers. I decided to donate my books to a couple local groups. Doug helped by getting my covers to the right size so I could take them to the local printing shop. To finish, I carefully glued each new cover onto the exposed pages. Yay! Now that was a first for me!

What I loved about this whole process, and why I'm sharing it with you, was how each organization came to me at just the right time. I met a particular person at the exact time I needed to. Now, I was ready (and able) to fulfill my dream. I was able to finally help someone.

One Way Farm Children's Home and The Dove House are the two local groups who help young women and children. My hope was that my gift would offer yet another tool to those who work so hard to help others. These organizations continue to make me think, "What else could I be doing?"

I ended this journey by speaking about abuse for The Dove House at our local federal building. I worked with the owner of One Way Farm, Barbara Condo, to edit and publish her book, You Don't

Know Where I Came From. Not bad results for the small gesture of offering some damaged books!

My point in sharing this story is awareness. When there is an issue you need to handle, look around you, get quiet, and wait to see what presents itself. The answer may not come right away, but in time, you will see an interaction of some sort. When you are being conscious, you'll notice it...the answer you need. Yes, you may be enlightened with a response from the universe!

In time, you will discover portions of your purpose. You'll recognize who you gravitate toward, who you might help, and why you meet certain people. There is always a reason. You only need to stay mindful, conscious, and intuitive.

Doug Heatherly, Lighthouse24: www.lighthouse24.com
The Dove House: www.ywcahamilton.com/domestic-violence
Barbara Condo, owner of One Way Farm Children's Home and author of You Don't Know Where I Came From: available on www.Amazon.com

CONSCIOUSLY GIVING AND RECEIVING

You have heard *it is better to give than to receive*, and that you shouldn't look to receive when you give to someone. We call that being a good person. Nevertheless, whenever possible, shouldn't you *expect* people to be grateful...and show it?

People offer their support all the time to those in need...and they should! It certainly is the way to be in this trying, and sometimes, entitled and selfish world. The only thing most of us want in return is a little gratitude; a nice smile, a genuine *thank you*, or a pat on the back to show appreciation for our service.

In most scenarios, those getting assistance should attempt to provide something in return; money, a bartering of service, or some sort of payback. Obviously, there are times when no return is possible. As for the rest of us, being *conscious* of our attitude and actions are what we need to nurture; in ourselves and each other. As I said before, we are all on this earth to be used, just not abused.

Anytime you offer service to another, God is with you; watching. The question is do *you* pay attention? Do those receiving your kindness pay any mind? When possible, do you receive a little kindness or appreciation for what you do? Yes, I know you aren't supposed to *expect* anything in return. But should you? If there's one thing I know with certainty, it's that people like to be appreciated.

Personally, I think it's a great trait to teach children, no matter if they are your kids or others. Just share! Make a big deal when a child does something nice for you. Offer your appreciation in a grandiose way so they know it's important.

There are homeless, abused, orphaned, and many other victims everywhere. Do you give to them if they show no signs of appreciation? Of course, you do! Why wouldn't you *expect* more from them? Because their situation may be so devastating, so sad, that they may not even realize they aren't giving back. They may not even know *how* to give back. Still, you give to them...without judgment. They are in need and you have it to give. The point is to stay conscious about what you give, who you give to, and why?

The Mindful, Intentional YOU

Aside from the whole *giving to the needy*, when do you decide that your giving outweighs what you receive in your relationships? Are you giving *consciously*, or are you randomly throwing out good deeds? Can you even identify what it is you do for others…and do you need to? Perhaps you're providing a service to someone, offering a warm touch, or a much needed compliment? Whatever you do, be *conscious* to whether you're doing enough and, just as important, doing what's right.

Let's explore the idea of helping those who are unwilling to help themselves? I did not say unable. I said *unwilling*. Those who take, take, take, and never give anything back. They see others as a means to an end; someone who has something to offer. They have the mindset that they can always fall back on someone else to pick up where they left off or messed up. And what you give is never enough. You have to wonder what you are proving; offering to those who are *not* in need. Not to mention, *why* you still give.

There are quite a few responses that come to mind, but let's try to narrow it down. Perhaps, you feel guilty about the past. Maybe you just can't say *no*. Then again, you simply don't mind helping anyone who asks. Or maybe you believe it is out of love, your desire to save the world, or it's basically how you were raised. Whatever the reason, the key is to know if you are doing the right thing. Are you being *conscious* with your good deeds?

Recognize if you are missing the real lesson. That is especially true when you are in a *teaching* moment. Should you *expect* something in return? Are they displaying gratitude? Is there a plan for them to help themselves? What happens if you are not there to provide the same service in the future? Are they able to take care of themselves? Are they *expecting* you to get them out of a hole they dug? Do they want you to rescue them, once again? Have you taught them anything in the process? So many questions! Honestly, the answers depend on what you are providing, what you *expect*, and what, if any, lesson is lost.

Nevertheless, there will always be *servers of the needy* who get taken advantage of in some way. Take the person who continually asks the church for help, while they continue to dine out, purchase big screen televisions, or buy alcohol or junk food with government cards. They may give more to themselves than they do their own family or friends. Who are they? They are the takers, and they need to be taught.

Still, it is God's will that we are servers of the people. Some do more and some do less, but doing God's work should be our number one priority. A true *server of the needy* will still give, without judgment, to each person standing in front of them. That is their purpose. They know God is always observing and *everything happens for a reason.*

So what good do you do by helping those who won't help themselves? Good question…and *food for thought* for you. As for me, I believe what goes around comes around. I don't worry too much in situations when I am helping the needy. Although it makes my heart sad to know someone would take advantage. I do, however, question my intentions when helping someone dear to me. I need to consider if they are continually making bad choices while constantly asking for my help? I have to ponder whether I'm really helping at all!

In summary, are you *conscious* of the choices you make when giving? Are you looking at the whole picture, or keeping it simple for everyone involved? I just want you to consider the idea that many times, being conscious and sharing lessons can stop the continued spiraling of bad choices…for them *and* you.

"It is more blessed to give than to receive." ~ Bible Acts 20:35 KJV

EVERYTHING AS IT SHOULD BE

Recently, I asked someone close to me how she handles these situations. You have to know that this is a woman who continually does everything for everyone...without getting much in return. She babysits for families, serves food at a nearby school, and offers help at the local senior center. For all that she does, she receives very little except (hopefully) a bit of gratitude. Obviously, all of her service up to this point sounds right with the world, doesn't it? I think so.

Now, add the fact that she has battled cancer, has a husband who underwent open heart surgery, takes care of the elderly and school children, and attends grief counseling with another family member. Not to mention, she lost a few family members of her own in the process! Sounds like an angel, doesn't she? I think so.

Still, I needed to know about those who take advantage of her service. Does she ever have to deal with takers? I asked her that question and her reply was simple. She said, "I don't look at it that way. My faith in God guides me and I know that everything works out as it should." She said God put her in a place where she is able to offer herself freely and that is her calling. She doesn't worry about whether someone is taking advantage of the system, or her, because she believes everything will take care of itself.

I envy this woman for her attitude and faith, and I don't know how she does it all. I tend to wonder if she doesn't deal with many takers in her purpose *because* she is doing God's work. Perhaps, He sends her those who truly are in need.

I know she has raised a good family, has an awesome husband, and she surrounds herself with family and friends who adore her. God has blessed her with the riches of goodness, and she continually gives that away...one person at a time. Imagine everyone being this strong and giving. The world would be a much better place.

The point of these *giving* stories is about having faith in God and in your relationships. You have to know you. You need to know what your expectations are, how you judge, and most importantly, the strength of your faith. While I know this woman freely gives, for me, it's about being *conscious* in your giving and receiving. Not stingy, not tit-for-tat, but *conscious* as to why and what services you provide and what gratitude you give and receive.

> *I understand why we need to be conscious in receiving,*
> *But why in our giving?*

To me, giving to someone who isn't doing what they can for them self, many times isn't helping them long term. I find it useful to understand the benefits and consequences of my service. Recognize if you are helping or actually hurting someone by being their provider. When it is all said and done, does what you do or don't do really matter to their personal growth and development? Are they showing gratitude and giving back in some way? Are you keeping them from *their* purpose? If you're providing out of love and care, and no harm comes to their personal enrichment, you're probably good to go. Of course, having a strong faith is vital to your success.

Being *conscious* about what you give and receive provides balance, valuable lessons, and self-awareness. All of which are good traits. Since there are those who will want to take more than their fair share, you need to know the reasons you do what you do. You need strong faith and the ability to make *conscious* choices.

In the end, you have to answer this question for yourself. If you are a giver, give generously and *consciously*. If you are a taker, realize what you aren't giving to others; at the very least, your gratitude. And if in fact *we reap what we sow*, perhaps we receive less by God's hand in the end. While I believe forgiveness has already been given to those who believe, no one really knows what's to come. I believe He loves everyone the same, He watches over us, and we should *consciously* make an effort to shine His light on others.

KILL THEM WITH KINDNESS

How do you make your life better? As a good friend of mine once said, "I like how you turned that frown upside down!"

One way to make life better is to figure out new ways to *kill them with kindness*. Offering a kind gesture to someone else ultimately gives you the boost. You'll be lifted by their appreciation, a returned favor, or maybe a blessing through someone or something else! Somewhere along the line you get paid back for your good deeds.

Here are a few special acts you can do to help others. Some are simple and even silly. While other acts might be a new thought for you. When appropriate, share your good deeds by telling others what you've accomplished. Not in a boastful way, but as encouragement for them to join in or consider what *they* could do. The more ideas you share, the better chance we have for more kindness in our world.

- ♥ If you begin your day with the phrase by Goethe: "Nothing is worth more than this day," you will discover every day has something unique and special to offer. This is one of the best gifts to give to someone else. Why? Because your positive attitude shows up in your interactions, facial expressions, and gratitude toward everything you see and do. You change, therefore your relationships change. You become the best part of you.
- ♥ If someone close to you needs to start making better choices, offer up your assistance. No matter if they are in a financial, weight, medical, relationship, or other struggle, you may be able to help. Of course, you don't want to stick your nose where it doesn't belong, but a good friend will always offer themselves up in a loving and kind way. Obviously, the circumstances make a difference, too. If someone has a fight with a family member or splurges on a one-time item, you probably want to mind your own business. But if someone is in harm's way, and they aren't helping themselves, try to get them help. You could save them from their demise.

- Look for ways to recycle. If you can't give up your paper plates, use plate holders so only one plate is used. Assign a particular trash can as "Recyclables Only," tossing all your cans, plastics, and junk mail into the designated areas. Perhaps you could share the clothes and reusable items that your family has outgrown. You could give them to a friend, school, or donation center. Whatever you decide to do to make a dent in the world's waste is counted. Even your smallest contribution makes a bigger difference.
- Stop whatever it is you are doing and make a plan to go pick up someone in need. Take them where they need to go. When someone can't get out of the house to run errands, your offer of assistance can mean so much to them. Help them to get a break from normal everyday life. Perhaps, they have no transportation. Worse yet, a disabling health reason. Whether you take them to the store, a doctor appointment, or out for a nice lunch, the day out will mean so much to them. Being stuck, with no way out, is disabling. Even more so than the reason they can't get out in the first place.
- Take someone's kid. No, not literally. Call up a friend or relative and ask when it's a good time to pick up their child for an afternoon of fun. You could go to lunch, to the park, or a special event. Give your loved one a break for a few hours. Maybe the whole day! Getting involved in their lives and caring about their child's well-being will be appreciated. The big plus is that you get to have a new experience through a child's eyes.

Now, head out into the world and make a difference for someone else.

TAKING A PERSONAL DAY

As you go through that list of all the work you have to accomplish, do you stop at the end of the day and realize you just gave away all of you…to work…again! You left nothing for play! Did you spend the last minutes of the day trying to shove in time that you should have spent with people who mean the most? By nightfall, you are probably pretty tired. You worked all day, got most of what you needed done, only to find that you are exhausted and didn't take any time to connect with anyone outside of the office.

When you're scheduling all of the responsibilities in your day, block out a piece of time to connect with someone outside of your work environment. While you might not get together at that very moment, a date can be made to do so in the near future.

When you get home, make a point, every day, to spend the first hour or two simply talking to those dearest to you; a mate, kids, your parents, or siblings. If no one is available, spend some quality time collecting yourself. Sit quietly, close your eyes, and reflect.

Meet a friend for lunch, show up at your child's school with pizza or cupcakes, or take your mate on a date! There are tons of ideas to show your gratitude to those you love. In addition to showing your love, you get the pleasure of having fun, too.

The reason you make a connection is to show someone special that *they* are special. You don't want to stick your face in the phone while trying to reconnect with them, and you don't want to be late. Their time is valuable, too. Being late or getting distracted by a device is rude and disrespectful. Make the time count.

Obviously, you'll have circumstances that don't make for a perfect environment every time. Still, the norm should be to think about the situation *before* you reconnect. Don't take that other call, make sure you're on time, and actually listen when conversation is flowing. If you are with someone for an hour, that incoming phone call can probably wait. However, if you plan on spending the day with them, chances are you may need to excuse yourself now and then. You know if you are being polite. You make the call.

When you take a personal day, that's what it should be; personal. Don't allow anyone to put you on hold unnecessarily, and don't do that to them. Be there…in the moment.

When you reach the end of your life, you won't be sorry you didn't work more hours or got more successful. You won't care that you didn't reach the top of your game. You will, however, be sorry that you didn't spend more quality time with loved ones; your family and friends.

Don't wait until the end of the day to schedule more time to be with those you care about the most. They may not be there the next time you have time.

THE IRON WORKER WHO MADE HIS WAY HOME

I share this particular story because it touched my heart so much. Every time I read it, I get chills up and down my spine. It reminds me of the relationships that have gone. Those wonderful people who I never get to see, but remain in my heart and mind on a regular basis. I share in hopes of offering peace to someone during their time of grief. I want them to relate to the beauty of God's everlasting place for us.

It was a few years ago when my husband and I paid our respects to a fallen family member. He was a young man who no one thought would leave this world so soon. I never met this man, but I knew many of my relatives were deeply saddened by their loss. And although I never knew him, I felt their pain and sorrow.

While we sat in church, we listened intently to the booming voice of the priest and the beautiful pitch of the singer. It was a moving service, and I was brought to tears by the words being spoken. At some point in the service, the priest asked God to show his face. I felt this oddly familiar; however, I didn't make it a habit to request this of God. I thought, "Perhaps I should start asking God to please show His face."

After the service, we followed the caravan of vehicles over to the gravesite. As we took our places, I looked up to see hundreds of birds swarming right above the burial site. They seemed to be flying in a circle or a figure eight. That's new! For me, birds are symbols that represent God more than other imageries. When I see a bird floating across the sky, I am reminded of just how big the universe is, and that God is always near. Still, the figure eight was new to me.

It was then that the chaplain approached and started to tell the story of a young man who went to Heaven. The man we were paying our respects to was an iron worker. This man's story was also about an iron worker so it fit perfectly for the occasion. I might have missed this moment had it not hit so close to home. It was in that very second that I started to put the pieces together.

The story was about an iron worker. The man we were saying goodbye to was an iron worker. And many of the people surrounding me at the service were iron workers; including my husband. If that wasn't enough, I realized my grandson's young father, who we buried only a few weeks before, was also an iron worker. I knew my grandson would appreciate this story.

Soon, the chaplain finished his sermon, we said our goodbyes, and we went down the street to gather for some food and prayer. It was then that the birds simply flew away.

Later, I approached the storytelling man to tell him how much I enjoyed his words. I wanted to know who wrote it so I could share it with my grandson. "I did...this morning," he said. Wow!

The end of this journey takes us to the widow; the woman who is left to pick up all the pieces. During the two times we approached her...to console her in her time of need...she ended up saying words that consoled us! Now that is powerful! She told us that her husband left her many gifts, but there was one very special gift he gave to her. He showed her that life didn't need to be that hard. She said, "He taught me that." What a beautiful gift to give and receive!

We were emotionally drained by the end of the day, but we wouldn't have missed being there. The spiritual connections we were given were immeasurable. Imagine...attending a funeral to support someone, then leaving with more support than you gave. That's how life works sometimes!

To conclude this story, I ended up connecting with the chaplain's editor; in hopes of getting his book off to a good start. We had only one conversation, but I felt privileged that it was me. I was helping another in their journey of writing.

I find it so interesting how intertwined people get at one time or another. The connections we make can be multilayered, and we meet them when we least expect it. First, I'm surrounded by iron workers; me, unaware of their bond. Next, I get to meet the man who told a wonderful story, which might help a young child with their own grief. Still later, I find I have something to offer in return...my writing skills. First, I am absorbed in hearing this man's story, then able to offer my assistance in return. That's a grateful moment.

When you consider how easily you could mold together or unravel and separate, based on how you treat each other, isn't it worth the effort to show kindness and respect to each other? Isn't it remarkable to know why something is happening *because* you are being mindful in your connections? To me, it's a magnificent gift to actually *see* the connection!

As I have said before, my motto is to not burn bridges. You never know where they may lead you. If I hadn't seen the connections, I would have missed out on so many of these blessings. None of us know how we could be connected to each other. You have to stay present…in the moment. So you don't miss out on a loving or spiritual connection. Stay connected.

Now, read on to discover the chaplain's story.

THE IRON WORKER WHO MADE HIS WAY HOME

There was a young man who died and went to Heaven. When he got there, he was greeted by an older white-haired gentleman who welcomed him in and offered to show him around the place.

The young man said, "That would be great."

As they walked through the gates, the young man noticed a very long path that led to what seemed like infinity. As they walked down that path, he began to see what looked like different sections.

The first section was an area where there were all kinds of skyscrapers and metal going up. There was steel being erected as far as the eye could see. The young man asked, "What is all of this?"

The older gentleman said, "This is the section for the local ironworkers. They get that in their blood and you can't get them to stop. The Creator knew He needed a place for them to do what they loved."

The next place they came to was a huge forest. There were trees as far as the eye could see.

The young man said, "This is so beautiful. I could spend years in here and never see all the different kind of trees."

The older man said, "Well, son, that is the point. This place is for those who love trees."

Soon, they came to a place just littered with ponds and lakes, with all kinds of people hunting and fishing.

The young man's eyes lit up as the older man said, "This is a place to come for those who love to hunt and fish."

The young man was taken aback by all of the beauty and the grandeur of it all. He could not believe his eyes.

He said, "Can I ask you a question?"

The older man said, "Sure."

The younger man said, "I thought that Heaven was made up of streets of gold and the mansions were so big and beautiful that no one would believe it. This doesn't look like that."

The older gentleman gave a long sigh and began to answer the young man's question. He said, "Son, the Creator of the universe would not be the creator if he did not know that everyone's idea of gold, silver, and mansions is different than everyone else's. One man's streets of gold and mansions might be a gravel road that leads to the greatest pond that ever was. That man would not be happy in a mansion with gold streets outside.

This is a place where people do not know pain and do not know bitterness and anger. This is a place where you will live for eternity doing the things you love to do.

Oh, and by the way, in a little while we are going to walk by the section where the streets are gold and the mansions are huge. We have to be really quiet when we do though because they think they are the only ones here."

The young man was so blown away by the solace in Heaven that he almost forgot how he got there. Then, just as quickly, he remembered how, but much to his surprise he was not sad. He looked puzzled at the older gentleman and the older gentleman knew that look. He had seen it many times before.

"There are a lot of people who are sad that you are gone, but this is not a place of sadness and you will never know that feeling exists."

The young man and the older gentleman parted ways with a firm handshake, and as their eyes met, the young man knew everything was going to be alright. He could start looking up loved ones and making new friends, while somehow, someway he knew inside that he would never forget those he left behind, and he knew that he could not feel sadness, but he was alright with that because he knew that the Creator of the universe would take care of them, just as He had taken care of him. He knew that while the sadness would never go away, and their lives would never be the same, he knew that each and every day, with the help of the Lord, the pain would ease, and one day their days would become bearable again. He could live eternity with that knowledge.

~ Chaplain Fuzzy Lake

8
The Audit of Your Attitude

"If I always do as I've always done,
I will always get what I've always got."
~ Author Unknown

AFTERTHOUGHT

Some people have been trained to always be *the one*. I am talking about the ones who take care of everything. They are the people-pleasers. I know this because I was one.

If I wasn't trying to stay on top of *all* of the details, I did things for others just out of guilt. I didn't want to let anyone down, and I wanted to be the best in their eyes. My boss, mate, or friend would ask me to do something and I was on it! Change is a coming!

Those days are over! Yes, I still do what I can to support my relationships, but I also take care of *my* needs. And that's okay! I don't have to do everything or be everything for everybody. I can just be me! I was born on this earth like everyone else. I deserve to get my needs met. And you deserve it, too. You cannot forget to take care of you.

This book has always been about you. I mean, that was my *intent* throughout my writing anyway…you. I spoke about other people and how you relate to them. I talked about who did what and how that changed you, but ultimately it was about you. Even in my personal stories, my hope was that you gained some clarity in your own life; through the actions of another.

Whatever you face, whoever comes your way, you have to decide to always do what is right…for you. Of course, you will care about others, and do for others, but since you only get one shot at life, you ought to make it good. While I encourage you to be the best you can be, give what you are able to others, and to be smart when dealing with other people, the real test is this: are you happy?

Are you putting *you* on the list? Do you value yourself enough to put you on the list? Do you know what you have to offer? Are you expecting enough, giving enough, and making conscious change for the better? I certainly hope so.

As you consider what and who makes you happy, you may find that you were always your best company. Friends and family are awesome; everyone needs someone. Still, the idea that *you* could be your true soul mate is interesting to me. I know I value my alone time. It gives me the opportunity to accomplish all that I want to do. I would bet you appreciate the time to get things done, too. The question is do you enjoy that time?

As you think about making change, everything comes down to how you react to it. It's good to think consciously, with intent, during various moments of the day. However, how you respond to problems greatly defines how much you've grown.

At this point, I hope you see that being intentional, conscious thinking, and mindfulness mean the same thing; a connection to life…as it unfolds around you.

The Mindful, Intentional YOU

With intention, you can create a *new* experience by focusing on the details. The realness of a flower, the varying sounds of nature, and, yes, by changing how you handle the outside forces coming at you. Look deeper at everything; even water, wind, and silence. Gaze deeply into someone's eyes as they speak to you, giving them all of your attention, as if you were looking at their soul. Show them you are in *listening* mode.

Finally, go out and live…in the moment! Take in each second, and know the choice has always been yours. The choice of what to say, do, think, and feel.

IN EVERY MOMENT, AN OPPORTUNITY TO AWAKEN

Each time you decide to become more conscious to what is going on around you, you are more awake. Every time you bring yourself back into a moment, you are *choosing* to be more purposeful.

Whether you are dating, in a marriage, or with family and friends, being able to bring your best self to the time together is a blessing for all. It's as easy as keeping your positive vibe alive. Acting more childlike at the family picnic might bring you inspiration. Playing ball or hide-and-seek with the kids could be your way of letting your hair down. Then again, sitting quietly while watching a bird fly to its nest might spark your intuitive interest. However you show up, do your best to stay present and in the moment. Make conscious choices through your thoughts and actions…and bring your best self.

When others pick up on your positive presence, an opportunity presents itself; allowing them to join in. They may begin to feel lighter, happier, and more at ease because of the energy you bring. Then again, they may not be present at all. Regardless of what happens around you, don't let it change how you react to the time together; stay with it. Set a good example of what it means to *live in the moment*. Even if no one else gets it, you do. You know how to see the beauty in the simplest of things.

Depending on how much positivity you take on, people around you might begin to wonder what is up with you. That's okay! Sometimes, when you start to think and live in a different way, there will be judgment. Those are the times when you must stay strong. Know you are putting your best self out there and you're happier for it. Keep them guessing as to why you are behaving in such a pleasant way.

Decide that you want to live this way…being more aware. Believe you have the power to enhance your relationships…through you. Most important of all, be the genuine you.

OUT OF TIME

A few years ago, someone sent this tale to me, and I wanted to share its insightful message with you.

Imagine you won a prize in a contest.
Each morning $86,400.00 would be deposited into your account to use however you want. However, this prize has rules; just as any game has certain rules.

The first set of rules would be:
- Everything you didn't spend that day would be taken away from you.
- You may not transfer money into another account; you can only spend it.
- Each morning upon awakening, your account is credited with another $86,400.00 just for that day.

The second set of rules:
The bank can end the game without warning; at any time. The bank can say, "It's over, the game is over!" It can close the account and you will not receive a new one.

What would *you* do?
- Would you buy anything and everything you wanted?
- Not only for you, but for all people you love?
- Even for people you don't know, because you know you couldn't possibly spend it all on yourself?
- You would try to spend every cent, and use it all, right?

Actually, this game *is* reality!

Each one of us is in possession of such a magical bank.
We just can't seem to see it.
The magical bank is time!

Each morning we awaken to receive 86,400 seconds as a gift of life, and when we go to sleep at night, any remaining time is not credited to us. What we haven't lived up that day is forever lost.

Yesterday is forever gone.

Each morning the account is refilled, but the bank can dissolve your account at any time...without warning!

So, what will *you* do with your 86,400 seconds?
Aren't they worth so much more than the same amount in dollars?

Think about that, and always think of this: Enjoy every second of your life, because time races by so much quicker than you think.

So take care of yourself, be happy, love deeply and enjoy life!

Author of story unknown

SEEKING TO UNDERSTAND

I wanted to end this book the way I started it. By explaining how I feel about thoughtfulness and understanding.

While I may have a mouth that doesn't always know when to hush, throughout the years, I have gained knowledge of the *think before you speak* rule. I know when I use the rule right, and I know when I've botched it all up.

> *"Seek first to understand, then to be understood."*
> ~ Stephen Covey

This is one of my most favorite quotes because I remember the first time I realized I wasn't following it. Not at all! We had a big event planned at work. Two famous coaches, Herman Boone and Bill Yoast were coming to corporate! They were the actual coaches based on the movie, *Remember the Titans*. I mean, who gets to do that! I felt so privileged to meet them.

My managers and I met them over breakfast and then came back to the facility to speak to our coworkers. After their speeches, they were to stay and take questions at the end. One speaker stayed while the other was no where to be found. This is where I got my wake-up call.

When I got back to the office, I made a judgemental comment to my coworker about the coach who left early from the event. I made some insulting remark about how he was supposed to stay after the talk and I couldn't believe he took off so fast.

This is when I was quickly put in my place.

My coworker informed me that the speaker was rushed to the hospital. He wanted to complete his duty, but he had felt bad all day and just couldn't stay any longer.

There it is! The exact moment when I remembered what I had studied in my class, Seven Habits of Highly Effective People: "Seek first to understand, then to be understood." Talk about being unaware in the moment!

If I had approached the situation with some hesitation in my judgment, I could have saved myself some embarrassment. Plus, my response would have been more thoughtful and kind.

Today, I love that I have become less judgmental about others. I find myself weighing options about what someone might have been thinking, or why their actions or words were not meant to harm. I do this before automatically deciding they are wrong. I see other sides of the equation, where before I could not.

Today, my hope is that I am helping others with the same issue. When I hear someone making allegations about another person, I find my mind, and mouth, sharing thoughts about other options that could be going on.

Still, at times, I make the mistake of not thinking matters through all the way. I spew my words all over the place. However, I know since *that* day I am more aware of my thoughts. Hopefully, most times, I have control over what comes out of my mouth.

www.movies.disney.com/remember-the-titans
www.stephencovey.com

The Mindful, Intentional YOU

YOUR PERSONAL AUDIT

When I read self-help books, I learn something new from all of the advice I receive. Still, I find I want to go directly to a few sections for key advice…at times when I need inspiration the most.

So, to make your time as productive as possible, I put together a few tips based on what you read…and more. Furthermore, don't forget your Top 20 Wish List *and* Standards, Expectations and Goals List. Those are important to complete.

When situations arise, or when you need some direction on staying conscious and intentional with your choices, look for guidance here. You will be pleased to know that reading over your created lists, and going through the tips below, can bring you back to a more foundational, conscious place.

Here are your tips:

- ♥ Don't pretend that you are anything other than yourself. Obviously, there are certain roles you play in life, but that shouldn't define you to the core. At times, you have to be that coworker, daughter, or mother. Other times, just a lover or friend. The key is to remember to always find your way back to the spiritual side of you.
- ♥ Don't doubt yourself. You are more than you know. If you think negative of yourself or criticize your worth, imagine that's what others will think of you, too.
- ♥ Live in the moments and stay aware of your surroundings. Start with nature because it's one of the easiest ways to connect. Then try to hear music…intentionally. If you feel the connection, turn to other substances, like running water or sharing an ice cream. Now, turn to looking, I mean *really* seeing your loved one as they talk to you. You will know what I am talking about when you *feel* the connection. You will experience your relationships in a very different way when your ego doesn't get in the way. You have probably heard the

aphorism, "The eyes are the window to the soul" by William Shakespeare. If you look close enough, you can see how true this is! Begin your day with a little reminder not to waste anymore of your time by not paying attention. This alone should make you more successful in all of your relationships because you'll capture the moments. And people will notice.

- You're entitled to be successful in everything you do, so long as you act with integrity and authenticity. That means, not stepping on anyone else in the process.
- Always wait until you're in a good mood before having important discussions with someone or when making big decisions. Why? Unless you're in harm's way, never make life changing choices while you're off balance. If you are sick, depressed, or angry…wait. Whether it's only a few days or weeks, it's important to wait to make good decisions. You have to pause until you're in the right frame of mind. You may not *feel* like your decision would be any different later, versus in the moment, but you'll see that when you make *conscious choices* you're exactly where you want and need to be…or not. You'll know you're making the right choice *because* you are thinking clearly.
- Keep your priorities straight, your standards and expectations high, and your desires fulfilled.
- Be assertive (not aggressive) in your relationships. You'll create a better atmosphere for you *and* them. By taking charge of your life, you remain true to yourself. Set some personal goals and make some plans.
- Even though your loved ones accept you as you are, you should still make an effort to improve yourself physically, mentally, and spiritually. True love tends to inhibit your sweetheart's perception so take that into consideration, too. None of us are as perfect as we think we are (chuckle).
- How do you know if you are where you're supposed to be? Well, you probably have the feeling that you see the path clearly, and the way to your future looks bright. Then again, if you feel weighed down, and are wondering how you even

landed here, you're situation may need some work? Decide why you should change it. Then, have enough perseverance to see the journey through. Nothing good is ever gained from aspects that come too easy. Remember, many times the answer isn't always the easiest path. If the situation (or relationship) is valuable to you, you'll work your way through the rough patches. If you determine your path is not what you want, have the courage to seek a new course.

- ♥ Figure out who and what makes you happy. Even if your situation isn't "the norm," if it makes *you* happy, then follow that dream. Don't get caught up in the harsh judgments and comments of others regarding your decisions. You choose what you want to keep and what you don't. Your decisions are yours to make.
- ♥ Understand that everyone has flaws. I'm not a perfect wife, mother, daughter, or friend. I don't have a perfect husband, son, sister, or father. No one does! Remind yourself of this fact during times of conflict. That will help get you through the disagreements and misunderstanding better.
- ♥ Forgive others for the mishaps, complaints, and old hurts they put upon you. Holding onto past pain is a waste of time and energy. Once you understand that a critical spirit leads to wasted days, you see the opportunity to start over. Then, you are able to adopt a new, positive attitude. And you won't waste one more day.
- ♥ You will have some hardships along the way. Get through them by focusing on your morals, values, and ending goals. At that point, do your best to turn around the areas that really matter.
- ♥ Speak the truth, even if it creates some difficulties. Especially, when you are standing up for what you require for yourself. You only control yourself and how you act (and react) in any given situation.
- ♥ Do your part in relationships and have a positive outlook for the future by staying focused. You will uncover your bliss directly from your own desires, actions, and expectations.

- ♥ Don't forget your personal well-being while you are getting ahead professionally. In the end, you will wish for more time with loved ones, but not for more time to work.
- ♥ Don't be a doormat. You can be a people-pleaser who helps whenever possible. Kindness and consideration should be part of your nature, but not to the point where your efforts are inappropriately expected.
- ♥ Never give up hope that the future will get better, and that change is possible. Don't be afraid of change or fear that you will fail during times of adjustment. Remember, it's only an adjustment.
- ♥ Take inventory of your own way of living to understand how you can contribute to a better society and better relationships.
- ♥ Finally, *be careful what you wish for…you just might get it.*

Okay, no excuses. Did you notice that the most meaningful gifts in life don't cost you a thing? Time and control are all you need. You need to take time when creating change, and you need to stay in control over how you handle situations. Both of which don't cost, but are most certainly priceless.

The best gift you can give yourself is realizing how worthy you are to be loved well. Love yourself through all of your challenges and triumphs. Ask for what you want out of life. If you fall back, don't get discouraged. Get up and start again. Everyone has bad days. Keep reaching toward your desires, and keep your values in place so you stay centered and moving forward. I ask you; please don't postpone your happiness any longer.

HELPFUL RESOURCES

BOOKS

The Seven Habits of Highly Effective People. Stephen R. Covey. Free Press. ISBN 978-0743269513

Smart Women Foolish Choices. Dr. Connell Cowan and Dr. Melvyn Kinder. Signet. ISBN 978-0451158857

Loving with Purpose. Kimberly Mitchell. White Orchid Publishing. ISBN 978-0982596401

Become a Better You. Joel Osteen. Free Press. ISBN 978-0743296885

A New Earth. Eckhart Tolle. Plume. ISBN 978-0452289963

The Purpose Driven Life. Rick Warren. Zondervan. ISBN 978-0310276999

Who *Moved My Cheese?* Spencer Johnson. Vermilion. ISBN 978-0091883768

Be on the lookout for my books on other topics; relationships, family, religion, and more. Go to www.lovingwithpurpose.org to learn more.

AUDIO AND VIDEO

Laugh Your Way to a Better Marriage. Mark Gungor. Crown Comedy. ASIN 1599754169

You Can Heal Your Life. Louise Hay. Hay House, Inc. ASIN B000Y04R96

The Secret. TS Production LLC. ASIN B000K8LV1O

WEBSITES/BLOGS

www.lovingwithpurpose.org
www.purposedrivenlife.com
www.eckharttolle.com
www.joycemeyer.org
www.joelosteen.com
www.louisehay.com
www.seatofthesoul.com
www.elizabethlesser.org

Any mention of these resources is given with the understanding that the publisher is not responsible for any use of any product, information, idea, or instruction contained in the contents provided to you.

To read more on *conscious* thinking, self-awareness, relationships, family and friends, check out my blog and book, Loving with Purpose. Or go to any of the following social media sites: Facebook, Twitter, Instagram, Pinterest, YouTube, Google, Tumblr.

KIMBERLY MITCHELL is the author of the books, *Loving with Purpose* and *The Mindful, Intentional You*. She is also the publisher of *The Heart of a Tiger*, *AfterWords*, and *You Don't Know Where I Came From*. She writes for venues such as her blog, *LovingwithPurpose.org*, Ezine articles, and other reputable sites offering advice.  As an entrepreneurial relationship contributor and a student of life, she believes that good or bad, personal experience is the best teacher. Her talents range from producing and presenting instructional material, building management and leadership courses, to personal development, diversity, and technical training. She also learned website creation and graphic design for company newsletters, brochures, websites, and educational material. Her work in human resources, along with her technical ability, provided her opportunities to combine those skills. All of which expanded her efforts to achieve success personally and professionally. Today, Kim has taken the long road of putting what she knows to paper. She has received so much more from the experience than she ever expected, and is thankful for the opportunity to contribute. Kim lives in Ohio with her husband, family members, and good friends. For more information, please visit *www.LovingwithPurpose.org*.

www.ingramcontent.com/pod-product-compliance
Lightning Source LLC
Chambersburg PA
CBHW071500040426
42444CB00008B/1432